A PILGRIM

K

CAMBRIDGE EDITION

A Pilgrim Family Devotional

for family & individual meditations, containing:

Robert Murray M'Cheyne's
DAILY BREAD

Charles Haddon Spurgeon's
A PURITAN CATECHISM

the
1742 PHILADELPHIA BAPTIST CONFESSION

and
SELECTED HYMNS & PSALMS

"Hear, O Israel: The LORD our God is one LORD: And thou shalt love the LORD thy God with all thine heart, and with all thy soul, and with all thy might. And these words, which I command thee this day, shall be in thine heart: And thou shalt teach them diligently unto thy children, and shalt talk of them when thou sittest in thine house, and when thou walkest by the way, and when thou liest down, and when thou risest up. And thou shalt bind them for a sign upon thine hand, and they shall be as frontlets between thine eyes. And thou shalt write them upon the posts of thy house, and on thy gates."

–DEUTERONOMY 6:4-9

compiled & edited by

JON J. CARDWELL

A Pilgrim Family Devotional
King James Version – Cambridge Edition

Published by Vayahiy Press

Printed by CreateSpace in the United States of America

CONTENTS

Catechism

Introduction and Instruction

C. H. Spurgeon's Introduction and Exhortation.

"I AM PERSUADED that the use of a good Catechism in all our families will be a great safeguard against the increasing errors of the times, and therefore I have compiled this little manual from the Westminster Assembly's and Baptist Catechisms, for the use of my own church and congregation. Those who use it in their families or classes must labour to explain the sense; but the words should be carefully learned by heart, for they will be understood better as years pass.

"May the Lord bless my dear friends and their families evermore, is the prayer of their loving Pastor."

—CHARLES H. SPURGEON
Pastor, Metropolitan Tabernacle
LONDON

J. J. Cardwell's Introduction and Instruction.

INTRODUCTION.

A Puritan Catechism was published about October 14, 1855, when Charles Spurgeon was just 21 years old. On October 14, Mr. Spurgeon preached "The Glorious Habitation" (Sermon No. 46) to thousands that gathered to hear him at New Park Street Chapel in Southwark. The text that morning was, *"Lord, thou hast been our dwelling place in all generations"* (Psalms 90:1). When the penny publication for this sermon was published it contained an announcement of this catechism.

INSTRUCTION.

With the centrality of God's Word so dear to the Puritans, one might think that we would begin with the Scripture readings from R. M. McCheyne's *Daily Bread* first. If you are so inclined, and moved within your soul by the Holy Spirit, by all means do so. What we have found to be very effectual for our family, however, is reciting portions of the catechism following our opening prayer; and then, reading our Scripture portions from the *Daily Bread* afterward. The reason for this, we have found for our family at least, is through the united recitation of the catechism, we seem to be more of one accord in our devotional family worship unto the Lord: Father reciting the question, and all in unison, reciting the answer to that question. This would be somewhat akin to a responsive reading in worship. Therefore, the Holy Scriptures may be better received when read.

Although there may be many possibilities with regard to parsing the recitation of the catechism, I have only two suggestions. You may actually choose something different from what I suggest; and that's quite alright.

1. Having 82 questions and answers, the family can recite 3 questions and answers each day, enabling you to complete the Catechism once in 27 days and 12 times each year. For the remaining days of the month, the family can read the Scripture proofs for 3 to 4 answers each day with the head of the family asking simple questions to clarify understanding. In this way, the Scripture proofs and doctrinal truths may be grasped more and more as each year passes.

2. The other method I might suggest would be to recite a page of the catechism each time you gather for devotions. For example, if you recite page 7 in the morning, recite the next page for devotions the following morning (that is, if you are using the Baptist Confession for reading during the evening devotions; otherwise, recite the next page during the evening devotions.

May our Lord bless you always in all ways as you grow in grace and faith.

JON J. CARDWELL.
Pastor, Sovereign Grace Baptist Church
ANNISTON, ALABAMA

A Puritan Catechism

"Study to shew thyself approved unto God, a workman that needeth not to be ashamed, rightly dividing the word of truth."

—2 Timothy 2:15

Q1. What is the chief end of man?
A. Man's chief end is to glorify God,[1] and to enjoy him forever.[2]

Q2. What rule has God given to direct us how we may glorify him?
A. The Word of God, which is contained in the Scriptures of the Old and New Testaments,[3] is the only rule to direct us how we may glorify God and enjoy him.[4]

Q3. What do the Scriptures principally teach?
A. The Scriptures principally teach what man is to believe concerning God, and what duty God requires of man.[5]

Q4. What is God?
A. God is a Spirit,[6] infinite,[7] eternal,[8] and unchangeable,[9] in his being,[10] wisdom, power,[11] holiness,[12] justice, goodness, and truth.[13]

Q5. Are there more Gods than one?
A. There is but one only,[14] the living and true God.[15]

Q6. How many persons are there in the Godhead?
A. There are three persons in the Godhead: the Father, the Son, and the Holy Ghost; and these three are one God, the same in substance, equal in power and glory.[16]

Q7. What are the decrees of God?
A. The decrees of God are his eternal purpose according to the counsel of his own will, whereby for his own glory he has foreordained whatsoever comes to pass.[17]

Q8. How doth God execute his decrees?
A. God executes his decrees in the works of creation[18] and providence.[19]

Q9. What is the work of creation?

A. The work of creation is God's making all things[20] of nothing, by the word of his power,[21] in the space of six days,[22] and all very good.[23]

Q10. How did God create man?
A. God created man, male and female, after his own image,[24] in knowledge, righteousness, and holiness,[25] with dominion over the creatures.[26]

Q11. What are God's works of providence?
A. God's works of providence are, his most holy,[27] wise,[28] and powerful[29] preserving and governing all his creatures, and all their actions.[30]

Q12. What special act of providence did God exercise towards man in the state wherein he was created?
A. When God had created man, he entered into a covenant of life with him, upon condition of perfect obedience;[31] forbidding him to eat of the tree of the knowledge of good and evil, upon pain of death.[32]

Q13. Did our first parents continue in the estate wherein they were created?
A. Our first parents, being left to the freedom of their own will, fell from that initial state wherein they were created, by sinning against God,[33] by eating the forbidden fruit.[34]

Q14. What is sin?
A. Sin is any want of conformity to, or transgression of the law of God.[35]

Q15. Did all mankind fall in Adam's first transgression?
A. The covenant being made with Adam, not only for himself, but for his posterity; all mankind, descending from him by ordinary generation, sinned in him, and fell with him, in his first transgression.[36]

Q16. Into what estate did the fall bring mankind?
A. The fall brought mankind into a state of sin and misery.[37]

Q17. Wherein consists the sinfulness of that state whereinto man fell?
A. The sinfulness of that state whereinto man fell consists in the guilt of Adam's first sin,[38] the want of original righteousness,[39] and the corruption of his whole nature, which is commonly called original sin;[40] together with all actual transgressions which proceed from it.[41]

Q18. What is the misery of that state whereinto man fell?
A. All mankind by their fall, lost communion with God,[42] are under his wrath and curse,[43] and so made liable to all the miseries in this life, to death itself, and to the pains of hell forever.[44]

Q19. Did God leave all mankind to perish in the state of sin and misery?
A. God, having out of his good pleasure from all eternity, elected some to everlasting life,[45] did enter into a covenant of grace to deliver them out of the state of sin and misery, and to bring them into a state of salvation by a Redeemer.[46]

Q20. Who is the Redeemer of God's elect?
A. The only Redeemer of God's elect is the Lord Jesus Christ,[47] who, being the eternal Son of God became man,[48] and so was, and continues to be God and man, in two distinct natures and one person, forever.[49]

Q21. How did Christ, being the Son of God, become man?
A. Christ, the Son of God, became man by taking to himself a true body,[50] and a reasonable soul,[51] being conceived by the power of the Holy Ghost in the virgin Mary, and born of her,[52] yet without sin.[53]

Q22. What offices does Christ execute as our Redeemer?

A. Christ, as our Redeemer, executes the offices of a prophet,[54] of a priest,[55] and of a king,[56] both in his state of humiliation and exaltation.

Q23. How does Christ execute the office of a prophet?
A. Christ executes the office of a prophet, in revealing to us,[57] by his Word[58] and Spirit,[59] the will of God for our salvation.

Q24. How does Christ execute the office of a priest?
A. Christ executes the office of a priest, in his once offering up of himself a sacrifice to satisfy divine justice,[60] and reconcile us to God,[61] and in making continual intercession for us.[62]

Q25. How does Christ execute the office of a king?
A. Christ executes the office of a king in subduing us to himself,[63] in ruling and defending us,[64] and in restraining and conquering all his and our enemies.

Q26. Wherein did Christ's humiliation consist?
A. Christ's humiliation consisted in his being born, and that in a low condition,[65] made under the law,[66] undergoing the miseries of this life,[67] the wrath of God,[68] and the cursed death of the cross;[69] in being buried, and continuing under the power of death for a time.[70]

Q27. Wherein consists Christ's exaltation?
A. Christ's exaltation consists in his rising again from the dead on the third day,[71] in ascending up into heaven, in sitting at the right hand of God the Father,[72] and in coming to judge the world at the last day.[73]

Q28. How are we made partakers of the redemption purchased by Christ?
A. We are made partakers of the redemption purchased by Christ, by the effectual application of it to us[74] by his Holy Spirit.[75]

Q29. How does the Spirit apply to us the redemption purchased by Christ?
A. The Spirit applies to us the redemption purchased by Christ, by working faith in us,[76] and thereby uniting us to Christ in our effectual calling.[77]

Q30. What is effectual calling?
A. Effectual calling is the work of God's Spirit,[78] whereby, convincing us of our sin and misery,[79] enlightening our minds in the knowledge of Christ,[80] and renewing our wills,[81] he does persuade and enable us to embrace Jesus Christ freely offered to us in the gospel.[82]

Q31. What benefits do they that are effectually called partake of in this life?
A. They that are effectually called do in this life partake of justification,[83] adoption,[84] and sanctification, and the several benefits which in this life do either accompany or flow from them.[85]

Q32. What is justification?
A. Justification is an act of God's free grace, wherein he pardons all our sins,[86] and accepts us as righteous in his sight,[87] only for the righteousness of Christ imputed to us,[88] and received by faith alone.[89]

Q33. What is adoption?
A. Adoption is an act of God's free grace,[90] whereby we are received into the number, and have a right to all the privileges, of the sons of God.[91]

Q34. What is sanctification?
A. Sanctification is the work of God's free grace,[92] whereby we are renewed in the whole man after the image of God,[93] and are enabled more and more to die unto sin, and live unto righteousness.[94]

Q35. What are the benefits which in this life do either accompany or flow from justification, adoption, and sanctification?
A. The benefits which in this life do accompany or flow from justification, adoption, and sanctification[95] are assurance of God's love, peace of conscience, joy in the Holy Ghost,[96] increase of grace, and perseverance therein to the end.[97]

Q36. What benefits do believers receive from Christ at death?
A. The souls of believers are at their death made perfect in holiness,[98] and do immediately pass into glory;[99] and their bodies, being still united in Christ,[100] do rest in their graves,[101] till the resurrection.[102]

Q37. What benefits do believers receive from Christ at the resurrection?
A. At the resurrection, believers, being raised up in glory,[103] shall be openly acknowledged and acquitted in the day of judgment,[104] and made perfectly blessed both in soul and body in the full enjoying of God[105] to all eternity.[106]

Q38. What shall be done to the wicked at their death?
A. The souls of the wicked shall at their death be cast into the torments of hell,[107] and their bodies lie in their graves till the resurrection and the judgment of the great day.[108]

Q39. What shall be done to the wicked at the day of judgment?
A. At the day of judgment the bodies of the wicked being raised out of their graves, shall be sentenced, together with their souls, to unspeakable torments with the devil and his angels for ever.[109]

Q40. What did God reveal to man for the rule of his disobedience?
A. The rule which God first revealed to man for his obedience is the moral law, which is summarized in the ten commandments.[110]

Q41. What is the sum of the ten commandments?
A. The sum of the ten commandments is to love the Lord our God with all our heart, with all our soul, with all our strength, and with all our mind; and our neighbor as ourselves.[111]

Q42. Which is the first commandment?
A. The first commandment is, *Thou shalt have no other gods before me.*[112]

Q43. What is required in the first commandment?
A. The first commandment requires us to know[113] and acknowledge God to be the only true God, and our God;[114] and to worship and glorify him accordingly.[115]

Q44. Which is the second commandment?
A. The second commandment is, *Thou shalt not make unto thee any graven image, or any likeness of anything that is in heaven above, or that is in the earth beneath, or that is in the water under the earth: Thou shalt not bow down thyself to them, nor serve them: for I the Lord thy God am a jealous God, visiting the iniquity of the fathers upon the children unto the third and fourth generation of them that hate me; and showing mercy unto thousands of them that love me, and keep my commandments.*[116]

Q45. What is required in the second commandment?
A. The second commandment requires the receiving, observing,[117] and keeping pure and entire, all such religious worship and ordinances as God hath appointed in his Word.[118]

Q46. What is forbidden in the second commandment?
A. The second commandment forbids the worshiping of God by images,[119] or any other way not appointed in his Word.[120]

Q47. Which is the third commandment?
A. The third commandment is, *Thou shalt not take the name of the Lord thy God in vain: for the Lord will not hold him guiltless that taketh his name in vain.*[121]

Q48. What is required in the third commandment?
A. The third commandment requires the holy and reverent use of God's names,[122] titles, attributes,[123] ordinances,[124] Word,[125] and works.[126]

Q49. Which is the fourth commandment?
A. The fourth commandment is, *Remember the sabbath day to keep it holy. Six days shalt thou labor, and do all thy work: but the seventh day is the sabbath of the Lord thy God: in it thou shalt not do any work, thou, nor thy son, nor thy daughter, thy manservant, nor thy maidservent, nor thy cattle, nor thy stranger that is within thy gates: For in six days the Lord made heaven and earth, the sea, and all that in them is, and rested the seventh day: wherefore the Lord blessed the sabbath day, and hallowed it.*[127]

Q50. What is required in the fourth commandment?
A. The fourth commandment requires the keeping holy to God such set times as he has appointed in his Word; expressly one whole day in seven, to be a holy sabbath to himself.[128]

Q51. How is the sabbath to be sanctified?
A. The sabbath is to be sanctified by a holy resting all that day, even from such worldly employments and recreations as are lawful on other days;[129] and spending the whole time in the public and private exercises of God's worship,[130] except so much as is to be taken up in the works of necessity and mercy.[131]

Q52. Which is the fifth commandment?
A. The fifth commandment is, *Honor thy father and thy mother: that thy days may be long upon the land which the Lord thy God giveth thee.*[132]

Q53. What is required in the fifth commandment?
A. The fifth commandment requires the preserving the honor, and performing the duties, belonging to everyone in their several places and relations, as superiors,[133] inferiors,[134] or equals.[135]

Q54. What is the reason annexed to the fifth commandment?
A. The reason annexed to the fifth commandment is, a promise of long life and prosperity— as far as it shall serve for God's glory and their own good— to all such as keep this commandment.[136]

Q55. Which is the sixth commandment?
A. The sixth commandment is, *Thou shalt not kill.*[137]

Q56. What is forbidden in the sixth commandment?
A. The sixth commandment forbids the taking away of our own life,[138] or the life of our neighbor unjustly,[139] or whatever tends to it.[140]

Q57. Which is the seventh commandment?
A. The seventh commandment is, *Thou shalt not commit adultery.*[141]

Q58. What is forbidden in the seventh commandment?
A. The seventh commandment forbids all unchaste thoughts,[142] words,[143] and actions.[144]

Q59. Which is the eighth commandment?
A. The eighth commandment is, *Thou shalt not steal.*[145]

Q60. What is forbidden in the eighth commandment?
A. The eighth commandment forbids whatever does, or may unjustly hinder our own,[146] or our neighbor's wealth or outward estate.[147]

Q61. Which is the ninth commandment?
A. The ninth commandment is, *Thou shalt not bear false witness against thy neighbor.*[148]

Q62. What is required in the ninth commandment?
A. The ninth commandment requires the maintaining and promoting of truth between man and man,[149] and of our own[150]

and our neighbor's good name,[151] especially in witness-bearing.[152]

Q63. Which is the tenth commandment?
A. The tenth commandment is, *Thou shalt not covet thy neighbor's house, thou shalt not covet thy neighbor's wife, nor his manservant, nor his maidservant, nor his ox, nor his ass, nor anything that is thy neighbor's.*[153]

Q64. What is forbidden in the tenth commandment?
A. The tenth commandment forbids all discontentment with our own estate,[154] envying or grieving at the good of our neighbor,[155] and all inordinate motions and affections to anything that is his.[156]

Q65. Is any man able perfectly to keep the commandments of God?
A. No mere man, since the fall, is able in this life perfectly to keep the commandments of God,[157] but doth daily break them in thought,[158] word,[159] and deed.[160]

Q66. Are all transgressions of the law equally heinous?
A. Some sins in themselves, and by reason of various aggravations, are more heinous in the sight of God than others.[161]

Q67. What does every sin deserve?
A. Every sin deserves God's wrath and curse, both in this life, and that which is to come.[162]

Q68. How may we may escape his wrath and curse due to us for sin?
A. To escape the wrath and curse of God due to us for sin, we must believe in the Lord Jesus Christ,[163] trusting alone to his blood and righteousness. This faith is attended by repentance for the past[164] and leads to holiness in the future.

Q69. What is faith in Jesus Christ?
A. Faith in Jesus Christ is a saving grace,[165] whereby we receive[166] and rest upon him alone for salvation,[167] as he is set forth in the gospel.[168]

Q70. What is repentance unto life?
A. Repentance unto life is a saving grace,[169] whereby a sinner, out of a true sense of his sin,[170] and apprehension of the mercy of God in Christ,[171] does with grief and hatred of his sin, turn from it unto God,[172] with full purpose to strive after new obedience.[173]

Q71. What are the outward means whereby the Holy Spirit communicates to us the benefits of redemption?
A. The outward and ordinary means whereby the Holy Spirit communicates to us the benefits of Christ's redemption, are the Word, by which souls are begotten to spiritual life; Baptism, the Lord's Supper, Prayer, and Meditation, by all which believers are further edified in their most holy faith.[174]

Q72. How is the Word made effectual to salvation?
A. The Spirit of God makes the reading, but especially the preaching of the Word, an effectual means of convicting and converting sinners,[175] and of building them up in holiness and comfort[176] through faith to salvation.[177]

Q73. How is the Word to be read and heard that it may become effectual to salvation?
A. That the Word may become effectual to salvation, we must attend to it with diligence,[178] preparation,[179] and prayer,[180] receive it with faith[181] and love,[182] lay it up into our hearts,[183] and practice it in our lives.[184]

Q74. How do Baptism and the Lord's Supper become spiritually helpful?
A. Baptism and the Lord's Supper become spiritually helpful, not from any virtue in them, or in him who does administer them,[185]

but only by the blessing of Christ,[186] and the working of the Spirit in those who by faith receive them.[187]

Q75. What is baptism?

A. Baptism is an ordinance of the New Testament, instituted by Jesus Christ,[188] to be to the person baptized a sign of his fellowship with him, in his death, and burial, and resurrection,[189] of his being ingrafted into him,[190] of remission of sins,[191] and of his giving up himself to God through Jesus Christ, to live and walk in newness of life.[192]

Q76. To whom is Baptism to be administered?

A. Baptism is to be administered to all those who actually profess repentance towards God,[193] and faith in our Lord Jesus Christ, and to none other.

Q77. Are the infants of such as are professing to be baptized?

A. The infants of such as are professing believers are not to be baptized because there is neither command nor example in the Holy Scriptures for their baptism.[194]

Q78. How is baptism rightly administered?

A. Baptism is rightly administered by immersion, or dipping the whole body of the person in water,[195] in the name of the Father, and of the Son, and of the Holy Spirit, according to Christ's institution, and the practice of the apostles,[196] and not by sprinkling or pouring of water, or dipping some part of the body, after the tradition of men.[197]

Q79. What is the duty of such as are rightly baptized?

A. It is the duty of such as are rightly baptized, to give themselves up to some particular and orderly Church of Jesus Christ,[198] that they may walk in all the commandments and ordinances of the Lord blameless.[199]

Q80. What is the Lord's Supper?
A. The Lord's Supper is an ordinance of the New Testament, instituted by Jesus Christ; wherein, by giving and receiving bread and wine, according to his appointment, his death is shown forth;[200] and the worthy receivers are, not after a corporeal and carnal manner, but by faith, made partakers of his body and blood, with all his benefits, to their spiritual nourishment, and growth in grace.[201]

Q81. What is required for the worthy receiving of the Lord's Supper?
A. It is required of them who would worthily partake of the Lord's Supper, that they examine themselves of their knowledge to discern the Lord's body,[202] of their faith to feed upon him,[203] of their repentance,[204] love,[205] and new obedience;[206] lest, coming unworthily, they eat and drink judgment to themselves.[207]

Q82. What is meant by the words, *"till he come,"* which are used by the apostle Paul in reference to the Lord's Supper?
A. They plainly teach us that our Lord Jesus Christ will come a second time; which is the joy and hope of all believers.[208]

---

[1] 1 Corinthians 10:31
[2] Psalm 73:25, 26
[3] Ephesians 2:20; 2 Timothy 3:16
[4] 1 John 1:3, 4
[5] Ecclesiastes 12:13; 2 Timothy 1:13
[6] John 4:24
[7] Job 11:7
[8] Psalm 90:2; 1 Timothy 1:17
[9] James 1:17
[10] Exodus 3:14
[11] Psalm 147:5
[12] Revelation 4:8
[13] Exodus 34:6, 7
[14] Deuteronomy 6:4
[15] Jeremiah 10:10

[16] Matthew 28:19; 1 John 5:7 (Although it is not included in newer translations such as the NIV, NLT, and etc., the KJV and the NKJV contain the following words that have been translated from the "majority texts" of the Greek manuscripts: *"For there are three that bear record in heaven, the Father, the Word, and the Holy Ghost: and these three are one."* There are certainly other passages that imply the triune Godhead in Scripture, i.e., the resurrection of Christ was accomplished by the Father (Ephesians 1:17-20), the Son (John 2:19), and the Holy Spirit (Romans 8:11). This doctrine is also referred to as "The Trinity.").
[17] Ephesians 1:11, 12
[18] Revelation 4:11
[19] Daniel 4:35
[20] Genesis 1:1
[21] Psalm 33:6, 9; Hebrews 11:3
[22] Exodus 20:11
[23] Genesis 1:31
[24] Genesis 1:27
[25] Ephesians 4:24; Colossians 3:10
[26] Genesis 1:28
[27] Psalm 145:17
[28] Isaiah 28:29
[29] Hebrews 1:3
[30] Psalm 103:19; Matthew 10:29
[31] Galatians 3:12
[32] Genesis 2:17
[33] Ecclesiastes 7:29
[34] Genesis 3:6-8
[35] 1 John 3:4
[36] Romans 5:12; 1 Corinthians 15:22
[37] Romans 5:18
[38] Romans 5:19
[39] Romans 3:10
[40] Psalm 51:5; Ephesians 2:1
[41] Matthew 15:19
[42] Genesis 3:8, 24
[43] Ephesians 2:3; Galatians 3:10
[44] Romans 6:23; Matthew 25:41
[45] 2 Thessalonians 2:13
[46] Romans 5:21
[47] 1 Timothy 2:5
[48] John 1:14
[49] 1 Timothy 3:16; Colossians 2:9
[50] Hebrews 2:14
[51] Matthew 26:38; Hebrews 4:15
[52] Luke 1:31, 35
[53] Hebrews 7:26
[54] Acts 3:22

---

[55] Hebrews 5:6
[56] Psalm 2:6
[57] John 1:18
[58] John 20:31
[59] John 14:26
[60] Hebrews 9:28
[61] Hebrews 2:17
[62] Hebrews 7:25
[63] Psalm 110:3
[64] Matthew 2:6: 1 Corinthians 15:25
[65] Luke 2:7
[66] Galatians 4:4
[67] Isaiah 53:3
[68] Matthew 27:46
[69] Philippians 2:8
[70] Matthew 12:40
[71] 1 Corinthians 15:4
[72] Mark 16:19
[73] Matthew 16:27; Acts 17:31
[74] John 1:12
[75] Titus 3:6, 6
[76] Ephesians 2:8
[77] Ephesians 3:17
[78] 2 Timothy 1:19
[79] Acts 2:37
[80] Acts 26:18
[81] Ezekiel 36:26, 27
[82] John 6:44, 45
[83] Romans 8:30
[84] Ephesians 1:5
[85]1 Corinthians 1:30
[86] Romans 3:24; Ephesians 1:7
[87] 2 Corinthians 5:21
[88] Romans 5:19
[89] Galatians 2:16; Philippians 3:9
[90] 1 John 3:1
[91] John 1:12; Romans 8:17
[92] 2 Thessalonians 2:13
[93] Ephesians 4:24
[94] Romans 6:11
[95] Romans 5:1-2, 5
[96] Romans 14:17
[97] Philippians 4:18; 1 Peter 1:5; 1 John 5:13
[98] Hebrews 12:23
[99] Luke 23:43; 2 Corinthians 5:8; Philippians 1:23
[100] 1 Thessalonians 4:14

[101] Isaiah 57:2
[102] Job 19:26
[103] 1 Corinthians 15:43
[104] Matthew 10:32
[105] 1 John 3:2
[106] 1 Thessalonians 4:17
[107] Luke 16:22-24
[108] Psalm 49:14
[109] Daniel 12:2; John 5:28, 29; 2 Thessalonians 1:9; Matthew 25:41
[110] Deuteronomy 10:4; Matthew 19:17
[111] Matthew 22:37-40
[112] Exodus 20:3
[113] 1 Chronicles 28:9
[114] Deuteronomy 26:17
[115] Matthew 4:10
[116] Exodus 20:4-6
[117] Deuteronomy 32:46; Matthew 28:20
[118] Deuteronomy 12:32
[119] Deuteronomy 4:15, 16
[120] Colossians 2:18
[121] Exodus 20:7
[122] Psalm 29:2
[123] Revelation 15:3, 4
[124] Ecclesiastes 5:1
[125] Psalm 138:2
[126] Job 36:24; Deuteronomy 28:58, 59
[127] Exodus 20:8-11
[128] Leviticus 19:30; Deuteronomy 5:12
[129] Leviticus 23:3
[130] Psalm 92:1, 2; Isaiah 58:13, 14
[131] Matthew 12:11, 12
[132] Exodus 20:12
[133] Romans 13:1; Ephesians 5:21, 22; Ephesians 6:1, 5
[134] Ephesians 6:9
[135] Romans 12:10
[136] Ephesians 6:2, 3
[137] Exodus 20:13
[138] Acts 16:28
[139] Genesis 9:6
[140] Proverbs 24:11, 12
[141] Exodus 20:14
[142] Matthew 5:28; Colossians 4:6
[143] Ephesians 5:4; 2 Timothy 2:22
[144] Ephesians 5:3
[145] Exodus 20:15
[146] 1 Timothy 5:8; Proverbs 28:19; Proverbs 21:6

[147] Ephesians 4:28
[148] Exodus 20:16
[149] Zechariah 8:16
[150] 1 Peter 3:16; Acts 25:10
[151] 3 John 12
[152] Proverbs 14:5, 25
[153] Exodus 20:17
[154] 1 Corinthians 10:10
[155] Galatians 5:26
[156] Colossians 3:5
[157] Ecclesiastes 7:20
[158] Genesis 8:21
[159] James 3:8
[160] James 3:2
[161] John 19:11; 1 John 5:15
[162] Ephesians 5:6; Psalm 11:6
[163] John 3:16
[164] Acts 20:21
[165] Hebrews 10:39
[166] John 1:12
[167] Philippians 3:9
[168] Isaiah 33:22
[169] Acts 11:18
[170] Acts 2:37
[171] Joel 2:13
[172] Jeremiah 31:18, 19
[173] Psalm 119:59
[174] Acts 2:41, 42; James 1:18
[175] Psalm 19:7
[176] 1 Thessalonians 1:6
[177] Romans 1:16
[178] Proverbs 8:34
[179] 1 Peter 2:1, 2
[180] Psalm 119:18
[181] Hebrews 4:2
[182] 2 Thessalonians 2:10
[183] Psalm 119:11
[184] Hebrews 4:2; James 1:25
[185] 1 Corinthians 3:7; 1 Peter 3:21
[186] 1 Corinthians 3:6
[187] 1 Corinthians 12:13
[188] Matthew 28:19
[189] Romans 6:3; Colossians 2:12
[190] Galatians 3:27
[191] Mark 1:4; Acts 22:16
[192] Acts 2:38-42; Acts 22:16; Romans 6:4, 5; Galatians 3:26, 27; 1 Peter 3:21

---

193 Acts 2:38; Matthew 3:6; Mark 16:16; Acts 8:12, 36, 37; Acts 10:47, 48
194 Exodus 23:13; Proverbs 30:6
195 Matthew 3:16; John 3:23
196 Matthew 28:19, 20
197 John 4:1, 2; Acts 8:38, 39
198 Acts 2:47; 9:26; 1 Peter 2:5
199 Luke 1:6
200 1 Corinthians 11:23-26
201 1 Corinthians 10:16
202 1 Corinthians 11:28, 29
203 2 Corinthians 13:5
204 1 Corinthians 11:31
205 1 Corinthians 11:18-20
206 1 Corinthians 5:8
207 1 Corinthians 11:27-29
208 Acts 1:11; 1 Corinthians 11:26; 1 Thessalonians 4:16

Daily Bread
Introduction and Instruction

J. J. Cardwell's Introduction.

"Daily Bread" was written by Robert Murray M'Cheyne for the congregation at St. Peter's Church in Dundee, Scotland, and was presented to them on December 30, 1842 for use at the beginning of the calendar year. Our source for the inclusion of his message and calendar comes from *Memoir and Remains of the Rev. Robert Murray M'Cheyne, Minister of St. Peter's Church in Dundee* by Andrew Bonar.

R. M. McCheyne's Instructions.

BEING A CALENDAR FOR READING THROUGH THE WORD OF GOD IN A YEAR.

"Thy word is very pure: therefore thy servant loveth it."

MY DEAR FLOCK,— The approach of another year stirs up within me new desires for your salvation, and for the growth of those of you who are saved. *"For God is my record, how greatly I long after you all in the bowels of Jesus Christ."* What the coming year is to bring forth, who can tell? There is plainly a weight lying on the spirits of all good men, and a looking for some strange work of judgment coming upon this land. There is need now to ask that solemn question: *"If in the land of peace, wherein thou trustedst, they wearied thee, then how wilt thou do in the swelling of Jordan?"*

Those believers will stand firmest who have no dependence upon self or upon creatures, but upon Jehovah our Righteousness. We must be driven more to our Bibles, and to the mercy seat, if we are to stand in the evil day. Then we shall be able to say, like David, *"The proud have had me greatly in derision: yet have I not declined from thy law." "Princes have persecuted me without a cause: but my heart standeth in awe of thy word."*

It has long been in my mind to prepare a scheme of Scripture reading, in which as many as were made willing by God might agree, so that the whole Bible might be read once by you in the year, and all might be feeding in the same portion of the green pasture at the same time.

I am quite aware that such a plan is accompanied with many...

DANGERS.

(1.) *Formality.* —We are such weak creatures that any regularly returning duty is apt to degenerate into a lifeless form. The tendency of reading the Word by a fixed rule may, in same minds, be to create this skeleton religion. This is to be the peculiar sin of the last days: *"Having a form of godliness, but denying the power thereof."* Guard against this. Let the calendar perish rather than this rust eat up your souls.

(2.) *Self-righteousness.* —Some, when they have devoted their set time to reading the Word, and accomplished their prescribed portion, may be tempted to look at themselves with self-complacency. Many, I am persuaded, are living without any divine work on their soul— unpardoned and unsanctified, and ready to perish— who spend their appointed times in secret and family devotion. This is going to hell with a lie in the right hand.

(3.) *Careless reading.* —Few *tremble* at the Word of God. Few, in reading it, hear the voice of Jehovah, which is full of majesty. Some, by having so large a portion, may be tempted to weary of it, as Israel did of the daily manna, saying, *"Our soul loatheth this light bread!"* and to read it in a slight and careless manner. This would be fearfully provoking to God. Take heed lest that word be true of you: *"Ye said also, Behold, what a weariness is it! and ye have snuffed at it, saith the LORD of hosts."*

(4.) *A yoke too heavy to bear.* —Some may engage in reading with alacrity for a time, and afterwards feel it a burden, grievous to be borne. They may find conscience dragging them through the appointed task without any relish of the heavenly food. If this be the case with any, throw aside the fetter, and feed at liberty in the sweet garden of God. My desire is not to cast a snare upon you, but to be a helper of your joy.

If there be so many dangers, why propose such a scheme at all? To this I answer, that the best things are accompanied with danger, as the fairest flowers are often gathered in the clefts of some dangerous precipice. Let us weigh…

THE ADVANTAGES.

(1.) *The whole Bible will be read through in an orderly manner in the course of a year.* —The Old Testament once, the New Testament and Psalms twice. I fear many of you never read the whole Bible; and yet it is all equally divine: *"All Scripture is given by inspiration of God, and is profitable for doctrine, for reproof, for correction, for instruction in righteousness: that the man of God may be perfect."* If we pass over some parts of Scripture, we shall be incomplete Christians.

(2.) *Time will not be wasted in choosing what portions to read.* —Often believers are at a loss to determine towards which part of the mountains of spices they should bend their steps. Here the question will be solved at once in a very simple manner.

(3.) *Parents will have a regular subject upon which to examine their children and servants.* —It is much to be desired that family worship were made more instructive than it generally is. The mere reading of the chapter is often too like water spilt on the ground. Let it be read by every member of the family beforehand, and then the meaning and application drawn out by simple question and answer. The calendar will be helpful in this. Friends, also, when they meet, will have a subject for profitable conversation in the portions read that day. The meaning of difficult passages may be inquired from the more judicious and ripe Christians, and the fragrance of simpler Scriptures spread abroad.

(4.) *The pastor will know in what part of the pasture the flock are feeding.* —He will thus be enabled to speak more suitably to them on the Sabbath; and both pastor and elders will be able to drop a word of light and comfort in visiting from house to house, which will be more readily responded to.

(5.) *The sweet bond of Christian love and unity will be strengthened.* —We shall be often led to think of those dear brothers and sisters in the Lord, here and elsewhere, who agree to join with us in reading these portions. We shall oftener be led to agree on earth, touching something we shall ask of God. We shall pray over the same promises, mourn over the same confessions, praise God in the same songs, and be nourished by the same words of eternal life.

CALENDAR DIRECTIONS.

1. The center column contains the day of the month. The two first columns contain the chapter to be read in the family. The two last columns contain the portions to be read in secret.
2. The head of the family should previously read over the chapter for family worship, and mark two or three of the most prominent verses, upon which he may dwell, asking a few simple questions.
3. Frequently the chapter named in the calendar for family reading might be read more suitably in secret; in which case the head of the family should intimate that it be read in private, and the chapter for secret reading may be used in the family.

4. The metrical version of the Psalms should be read or sung through at least once in the year. It is truly an admirable translation from the Hebrew, and is frequently more correct than the prose version. If three verses be sung at each diet of family worship, the whole Psalms will be sung though in the year.

5. Let the conversation at family meals often turn upon the chapter read and the psalm sung. Thus every meal will be a sacrament, being sanctified by the Word and prayer.

6. Let our secret reading prevent the dawning of the day. Let God's voice be the first we hear in the morning. Mark two or three of the richest verses, and pray over every line and word of them. Let the marks be neatly done, never so as to abuse a copy of the Bible.

7. In meeting believers on the street or elsewhere, when an easy opportunity offers, recur to the chapters read that morning. This will be a blessed exchange for those *idle words* which waste the soul and grieve the Holy Spirit of God. In writing letters to those at a distance, make use of the provision that day gathered.

8. Above all, use the Word as a lamp to your feet and a light to your path— your guide in perplexity, your armour in temptation, your food in times of faintness. Hear the constant cry of the great Intercessor,

"SANCTIFY THEM THROUGH THY TRUTH: THY WORD IS TRUTH."

Rev. R.M. M'Cheyne
ST PETER'S, DUNDEE, *30th Dec.* 1842

JANUARY

THIS IS MY BELOVED SON, IN WHOM I AM WELL PLEASED; HEAR YE HIM.

FAMILY			SECRET	
Genesis 1	Matthew 1	**1**	Ezra 1	Acts 1
Genesis 2	Matthew 2	**2**	Ezra 2	Acts 2
Genesis 3	Matthew 3	**3**	Ezra 3	Acts 3
Genesis 4	Matthew 4	**4**	Ezra 4	Acts 4
Genesis 5	Matthew 5	**5**	Ezra 5	Acts 5
Genesis 6	Matthew 6	**6**	Ezra 6	Acts 6
Genesis 7	Matthew 7	**7**	Ezra 7	Acts 7
Genesis 8	Matthew 8	**8**	Ezra 8	Acts 8
Genesis 9-10	Matthew 9	**9**	Ezra 9	Acts 9
Genesis 11	Matthew 10	**10**	Ezra 10	Acts 10
Genesis 12	Matthew 11	**11**	Nehemiah 1	Acts 11
Genesis 13	Matthew 12	**12**	Nehemiah 2	Acts 12
Genesis 14	Matthew 13	**13**	Nehemiah 3	Acts 13
Genesis 15	Matthew 14	**14**	Nehemiah 4	Acts 14
Genesis 16	Matthew 15	**15**	Nehemiah 5	Acts 15
Genesis 17	Matthew 16	**16**	Nehemiah 6	Acts 16
Genesis 18	Matthew 17	**17**	Nehemiah 7	Acts 17
Genesis 19	Matthew 18	**18**	Nehemiah 8	Acts 18
Genesis 20	Matthew 19	**19**	Nehemiah 9	Acts 19
Genesis 21	Matthew 20	**20**	Nehemiah 10	Acts 20
Genesis 22	Matthew 21	**21**	Nehemiah 11	Acts 21
Genesis 23	Matthew 22	**22**	Nehemiah 12	Acts 22
Genesis 24	Matthew 23	**23**	Nehemiah 13	Acts 23
Genesis 25	Matthew 24	**24**	Esther 1	Acts 24
Genesis 26	Matthew 25	**25**	Esther 2	Acts 25
Genesis 27	Matthew 26	**26**	Esther 3	Acts 26
Genesis 28	Matthew 27	**27**	Esther 4	Acts 27
Genesis 29	Matthew 28	**28**	Esther 5	Acts 28
Genesis 30	Mark 1	**29**	Esther 6	Romans 1
Genesis 31	Mark 2	**30**	Esther 7	Romans 2
Genesis 32	Mark 3	**31**	Esther 8	Romans 3

FEBRUARY

I HAVE ESTEEMED THE WORDS OF HIS MOUTH MORE THAN MY NECESSARY FOOD.

FAMILY			SECRET	
Genesis 33	Mark 4	**1**	Esther 9-10	Romans 4
Genesis 34	Mark 5	**2**	Job 1	Romans 5
Genesis 35-36	Mark 6	**3**	Job 2	Romans 6
Genesis 37	Mark 7	**4**	Job 3	Romans 7
Genesis 38	Mark 8	**5**	Job 4	Romans 8
Genesis 39	Mark 9	**6**	Job 5	Romans 9
Genesis 40	Mark 10	**7**	Job 6	Romans 10
Genesis 41	Mark 11	**8**	Job 7	Romans 11
Genesis 42	Mark 12	**9**	Job 8	Romans 12
Genesis 43	Mark 13	**10**	Job 9	Romans 13
Genesis 44	Mark 14	**11**	Job 10	Romans 14
Genesis 45	Mark 15	**12**	Job 11	Romans 15
Genesis 46	Mark 16	**13**	Job 12	Romans 16
Genesis 47	Luke 1:1-38	**14**	Job 13	1 Cor. 1
Genesis 48	Luke 1:39-80	**15**	Job 14	1 Cor. 2
Genesis 49	Luke 2	**16**	Job 15	1 Cor. 3
Genesis 50	Luke 3	**17**	Job 16-17	1 Cor. 4
Exodus 1	Luke 4	**18**	Job 18	1 Cor. 5
Exodus 2	Luke 5	**19**	Job 19	1 Cor. 6
Exodus 3	Luke 6	**20**	Job 20	1 Cor. 7
Exodus 4	Luke 7	**21**	Job 21	1 Cor. 8
Exodus 5	Luke 8	**22**	Job 22	1 Cor. 9
Exodus 6	Luke 9	**23**	Job 23	1 Cor. 10
Exodus 7	Luke 10	**24**	Job 24	1 Cor. 11
Exodus 8	Luke 11	**25**	Job 25-26	1 Cor. 12
Exodus 9	Luke 12	**26**	Job 27	1 Cor. 13
Exodus 10	Luke 13	**27**	Job 28	1 Cor. 14
Ex. 11-12:21	Luke 14	**28**	Job 29	1 Cor. 15

Abbreviations: Ex. – Exodus; 1 Cor. – 1 Corinthians

LEAP YEAR - FEBRUARY/MARCH

FAMILY			SECRET	
Exodus 11	Luke 14:1-14	**28**	Job 29	1 Cor. 15:1-29
Exodus 12:1-21	Luke 14:15	**29**	Job 30:1-15	1 Cor. 15:30
Exodus 12:22	Luke 15	**1**	Job 30:16	1 Cor. 16

MARCH

BUT MARY KEPT ALL THESE THINGS, AND PONDERED THEM IN HER HEART.

FAMILY			SECRET	
Exodus 12:22	Luke 15	**1**	Job 30	1 Cor. 16
Exodus 13	Luke 16	**2**	Job 31	2 Cor. 1
Exodus 14	Luke 17	**3**	Job 32	2 Cor. 2
Exodus 15	Luke 18	**4**	Job 33	2 Cor. 3
Exodus 16	Luke 19	**5**	Job 34	2 Cor. 4
Exodus 17	Luke 20	**6**	Job 35	2 Cor. 5
Exodus 18	Luke 21	**7**	Job 36	2 Cor. 6
Exodus 19	Luke 22	**8**	Job 37	2 Cor. 7
Exodus 20	Luke 23	**9**	Job 38	2 Cor. 8
Exodus 21	Luke 24	**10**	Job 39	2 Cor. 9
Exodus 22	John 1	**11**	Job 40	2 Cor. 10
Exodus 23	John 2	**12**	Job 41	2 Cor. 11
Exodus 24	John 3	**13**	Job 42	2 Cor. 12
Exodus 25	John 4	**14**	Proverbs 1	2 Cor. 13
Exodus 26	John 5	**15**	Proverbs 2	Galatians 1
Exodus 27	John 6	**16**	Proverbs 3	Galatians 2
Exodus 28	John 7	**17**	Proverbs 4	Galatians 3
Exodus 29	John 8	**18**	Proverbs 5	Galatians 4
Exodus 30	John 9	**19**	Proverbs 6	Galatians 5
Exodus 31	John 10	**20**	Proverbs 7	Galatians 6
Exodus 32	John 11	**21**	Proverbs 8	Ephesians 1
Exodus 33	John 12	**22**	Proverbs 9	Ephesians 2
Exodus 34	John 13	**23**	Proverbs 10	Ephesians 3
Exodus 35	John 14	**24**	Proverbs 11	Ephesians 4
Exodus 36	John 15	**25**	Proverbs 12	Ephesians 5
Exodus 37	John 16	**26**	Proverbs 13	Ephesians 6
Exodus 38	John 17	**27**	Proverbs 14	Phil. 1
Exodus 39	John 18	**28**	Proverbs 15	Phil. 2
Exodus 40	John 19	**29**	Proverbs 16	Phil. 3
Leviticus 1	John 20	**30**	Proverbs 17	Phil. 4
Leviticus 2-3	John 21	**31**	Proverbs 18	Colossians 1

Abbreviations: 1 Cor. – 1 Corinthians; 2 Cor. – 2 Corinthians; Phil. – Philippians

APRIL

O SEND OUT THY LIGHT AND THY TRUTH: LET THEM LEAD ME.

FAMILY			SECRET	
Leviticus 4	Psalms 1-2	**1**	Proverbs 19	Colossians 2
Leviticus 5	Psalms 3-4	**2**	Proverbs 20	Colossians 3
Leviticus 6	Psalms 5-6	**3**	Proverbs 21	Colossians 4
Leviticus 7	Psalms 7-8	**4**	Proverbs 22	1 Thess. 1
Leviticus 8	Psalms 9	**5**	Proverbs 23	1 Thess. 2
Leviticus 9	Psalms 10	**6**	Proverbs 24	1 Thess. 3
Leviticus 10	Psalms 11-12	**7**	Proverbs 25	1 Thess. 4
Lev. 11-12	Psalms 13-14	**8**	Proverbs 26	1 Thess. 5
Leviticus 13	Psalms 15-16	**9**	Proverbs 27	2 Thess. 1
Leviticus 14	Psalms 17	**10**	Proverbs 28	2 Thess. 2
Leviticus 15	Psalms 18	**11**	Proverbs 29	2 Thess. 3
Leviticus 16	Psalms 19	**12**	Proverbs 30	1 Timothy 1
Leviticus 17	Psalms 20-21	**13**	Proverbs 31	1 Timothy 2
Leviticus 18	Psalms 22	**14**	Eccles. 1	1 Timothy 3
Leviticus 19	Psalms 23-24	**15**	Eccles. 2	1 Timothy 4
Leviticus 20	Psalms 25	**16**	Eccles. 3	1 Timothy 5
Leviticus 21	Psalms 26-27	**17**	Eccles. 4	1 Timothy 6
Leviticus 22	Psalms 28-29	**18**	Eccles. 5	2 Timothy 1
Leviticus 23	Psalms 30	**19**	Eccles. 6	2 Timothy 2
Leviticus 24	Psalms 31	**20**	Eccles. 7	2 Timothy 3
Leviticus 25	Psalms 32	**21**	Eccles. 8	2 Timothy 4
Leviticus 26	Psalms 33	**22**	Eccles. 9	Titus 1
Leviticus 27	Psalms 34	**23**	Eccles. 10	Titus 2
Numbers 1	Psalms 35	**24**	Eccles. 11	Titus 3
Numbers 2	Psalms 36	**25**	Eccles. 12	Philemon
Numbers 3	Psalms 37	**26**	Song. 1	Hebrews 1
Numbers 4	Psalms 38	**27**	Song. 2	Hebrews 2
Numbers 5	Psalms 39	**28**	Song. 3	Hebrews 3
Numbers 6	Psalms 40-41	**29**	Song. 4	Hebrews 4
Numbers 7	Psalms 42-43	**30**	Song. 5	Hebrews 5

Abbreviations: 1 Thess. – 1 Thessalonians; Lev. – Leviticus;
2 Thess. – 2 Thessalonians; Eccles. – Ecclesiastes;
Song. – Song of Solomon

MAY

FROM A CHILD THOU HAST KNOWN THE HOLY SCRIPTURES.

FAMILY			SECRET	
Numbers 8	Psalms 44	**1**	Song. 6	Hebrews 6
Numbers 9	Psalms 45	**2**	Song. 7	Hebrews 7
Numbers 10	Psalms 46-47	**3**	Song. 8	Hebrews 8
Numbers 11	Psalms 48	**4**	Isaiah 1	Hebrews 9
Numb. 12-13	Psalms 49	**5**	Isaiah 2	Hebrews 10
Numbers 14	Psalms 50	**6**	Isaiah 3-4	Hebrews 11
Numbers 15	Psalms 51	**7**	Isaiah 5	Hebrews 12
Numbers 16	Psalms 52-54	**8**	Isaiah 6	Hebrews 13
Numb. 17-18	Psalms 55	**9**	Isaiah 7	James 1
Numbers 19	Psalms 56-57	**10**	Isaiah 8:1-9:7	James 2
Numbers 20	Psalms 58-59	**11**	Isa. 9:8-10:4	James 3
Numbers 21	Psalms 60-61	**12**	Isaiah 10:5	James 4
Numbers 22	Psalms 62-63	**13**	Isaiah 11-12	James 5
Numbers 23	Psalms 64-65	**14**	Isaiah 13	1 Peter 1
Numbers 24	Psalms 66-67	**15**	Isaiah 14	1 Peter 2
Numbers 25	Psalms 68	**16**	Isaiah 15	1 Peter 3
Numbers 26	Psalms 69	**17**	Isaiah 16	1 Peter 4
Numbers 27	Psalms 70-71	**18**	Isaiah 17-18	1 Peter 5
Numbers 28	Psalms 72	**19**	Isaiah 19-20	2 Peter 1
Numbers 29	Psalms 73	**20**	Isaiah 21	2 Peter 2
Numbers 30	Psalms 74	**21**	Isaiah 22	2 Peter 3
Numbers 31	Psalms 75-76	**22**	Isaiah 23	1 John 1
Numbers 32	Psalms 77	**23**	Isaiah 24	1 John 2
Numbers 33	Psalms 78:1-37	**24**	Isaiah 25	1 John 3
Numbers 34	Psalms 78:38	**25**	Isaiah 26	1 John 4
Numbers 35	Psalms 79	**26**	Isaiah 27	1 John 5
Numbers 36	Psalms 80	**27**	Isaiah 28	2 John
Deut. 1	Psalms 81-82	**28**	Isaiah 29	3 John
Deut. 2	Psalms 83-84	**29**	Isaiah 30	Jude
Deut. 3	Psalms 85	**30**	Isaiah 31	Revelation 1
Deut. 4	Psalms 86-87	**31**	Isaiah 32	Revelation 2

Abbreviations: Numb. – Numbers; Deut. – Deuteronomy; Isa. – Isaiah

JUNE

BLESSED IS HE THAT READETH, AND THEY THAT HEAR.

FAMILY			SECRET	
Deut. 5	Psalms 88	**1**	Isaiah 33	Revelation 3
Deut. 6	Psalms 89	**2**	Isaiah 34	Revelation 4
Deut. 7	Psalms 90	**3**	Isaiah 35	Revelation 5
Deut. 8	Psalms 91	**4**	Isaiah 36	Revelation 6
Deut. 9	Ps. 92-93	**5**	Isaiah 37	Revelation 7
Deut. 10	Psalms 94	**6**	Isaiah 38	Revelation 8
Deut. 11	Ps. 95-96	**7**	Isaiah 39	Revelation 9
Deut. 12	Ps. 97-98	**8**	Isaiah 40	Rev. 10
Deut. 13-14	Ps. 99-101	**9**	Isaiah 41	Rev. 11
Deut. 15	Psalms 102	**10**	Isaiah 42	Rev. 12
Deut. 16	Psalms 103	**11**	Isaiah 43	Rev. 13
Deut. 17	Psalms 104	**12**	Isaiah 44	Rev. 14
Deut. 18	Psalms 105	**13**	Isaiah 45	Rev. 15
Deut. 19	Psalms 106	**14**	Isaiah 46	Rev. 16
Deut. 20	Psalms 107	**15**	Isaiah 47	Rev. 17
Deut. 21	Ps. 108-109	**16**	Isaiah 48	Rev. 18
Deut. 22	Ps. 110-111	**17**	Isaiah 49	Rev. 19
Deut. 23	Ps. 112-113	**18**	Isaiah 50	Rev. 20
Deut. 24	Ps. 114-115	**19**	Isaiah 51	Rev. 21
Deut. 25	Psalms 116	**20**	Isaiah 52	Rev. 22
Deut. 26	Ps. 117-118	**21**	Isaiah 53	Matthew 1
Deut. 27-28:19	119:1-24	**22**	Isaiah 54	Matthew 2
Deut. 28:20	119:25-48	**23**	Isaiah 55	Matthew 3
Deut. 29	119:49-72	**24**	Isaiah 56	Matthew 4
Deut. 30	119:73-96	**25**	Isaiah 57	Matthew 5
Deut. 31	119:97-120	**26**	Isaiah 58	Matthew 6
Deut. 32	119:121-144	**27**	Isaiah 59	Matthew 7
Deut. 33-34	119:145-176	**28**	Isaiah 60	Matthew 8
Joshua 1	Ps. 120-122	**29**	Isaiah 61	Matthew 9
Joshua 2	Ps. 123-125	**30**	Isaiah 62	Matthew 10

Abbreviations: Deut. – Deuteronomy; Ps. – Psalms; Rev. – Revelation

JULY

THEY RECEIVED THE WORD WITH ALL READINESS OF MIND, AND SEARCHED THE SCRIPTURES DAILY.

FAMILY			SECRET	
Joshua 3	Ps. 126-128	**1**	Isaiah 63	Matthew 11
Joshua 4	Ps. 129-131	**2**	Isaiah 64	Matthew 12
Joshua 5-6:5	Ps. 132-134	**3**	Isaiah 65	Matthew 13
Joshua 6:6	Ps. 135-136	**4**	Isaiah 66	Matthew 14
Joshua 7	Ps. 137-138	**5**	Jeremiah 1	Matthew 15
Joshua 8	Ps. 139	**6**	Jeremiah 2	Matthew 16
Joshua 9	Ps. 140-141	**7**	Jeremiah 3	Matthew 17
Joshua 10	Ps. 142-143	**8**	Jeremiah 4	Matthew 18
Joshua 11	Ps. 144	**9**	Jeremiah 5	Matthew 19
Joshua 12-13	Ps. 145	**10**	Jeremiah 6	Matthew 20
Joshua 14-15	Ps. 146-147	**11**	Jeremiah 7	Matthew 21
Joshua 16-17	Ps. 148	**12**	Jeremiah 8	Matthew 22
Joshua 18-19	Ps. 149-150	**13**	Jeremiah 9	Matthew 23
Joshua 20-21	Acts 1	**14**	Jeremiah 10	Matthew 24
Joshua 22	Acts 2	**15**	Jeremiah 11	Matthew 25
Joshua 23	Acts 3	**16**	Jeremiah 12	Matthew 26
Joshua 24	Acts 4	**17**	Jeremiah 13	Matthew 27
Judges 1	Acts 5	**18**	Jeremiah 14	Matthew 28
Judges 2	Acts 6	**19**	Jeremiah 15	Mark 1
Judges 3	Acts 7	**20**	Jeremiah 16	Mark 2
Judges 4	Acts 8	**21**	Jeremiah 17	Mark 3
Judges 5	Acts 9	**22**	Jeremiah 18	Mark 4
Judges 6	Acts 10	**23**	Jeremiah 19	Mark 5
Judges 7	Acts 11	**24**	Jeremiah 20	Mark 6
Judges 8	Acts 12	**25**	Jeremiah 21	Mark 7
Judges 9	Acts 13	**26**	Jeremiah 22	Mark 8
Jud. 10-11:11	Acts 14	**27**	Jeremiah 23	Mark 9
Judges 11:12	Acts 15	**28**	Jeremiah 24	Mark 10
Judges 12	Acts 16	**29**	Jeremiah 25	Mark 11
Judges 13	Acts 17	**30**	Jeremiah 26	Mark 12
Judges 14	Acts 18	**31**	Jeremiah 27	Mark 13

Abbreviations: Ps. – Psalms; Jud. – Judges

AUGUST

SPEAK, LORD; FOR THY SERVANT HEARETH.

FAMILY			SECRET	
Judges 15	Acts 19	**1**	Jeremiah 28	Mark 14
Judges 16	Acts 20	**2**	Jeremiah 29	Mark 15
Judges 17	Acts 21	**3**	Jer. 30-31	Mark 16
Judges 18	Acts 22	**4**	Jeremiah 32	Psalms 1-2
Judges 19	Acts 23	**5**	Jeremiah 33	Psalms 3-4
Judges 20	Acts 24	**6**	Jeremiah 34	Psalms 5-6
Judges 21	Acts 25	**7**	Jeremiah 35	Psalms 7-8
Ruth 1	Acts 26	**8**	Jer. 36-45	Psalms 9
Ruth 2	Acts 27	**9**	Jeremiah 37	Psalms 10
Ruth 3-4	Acts 28	**10**	Jeremiah 38	Psalms 11-12
1 Samuel 1	Romans 1	**11**	Jeremiah 39	Psalms 13-14
1 Samuel 2	Romans 2	**12**	Jeremiah 40	Psalms 15-16
1 Samuel 3	Romans 3	**13**	Jeremiah 41	Psalms 17
1 Samuel 4	Romans 4	**14**	Jeremiah 42	Psalms 18
1 Samuel 5-6	Romans 5	**15**	Jeremiah 43	Psalms 19
1 Samuel 7-8	Romans 6	**16**	Jeremiah 44	Psalms 20-21
1 Samuel 9	Romans 7	**17**	Jeremiah 46	Psalms 22
1 Samuel 10	Romans 8	**18**	Jeremiah 47	Psalms 23-24
1 Samuel 11	Romans 9	**19**	Jeremiah 48	Psalms 25
1 Samuel 12	Romans 10	**20**	Jeremiah 49	Psalms 26-27
1 Samuel 13	Romans 11	**21**	Jeremiah 50	Psalms 28-29
1 Samuel 14	Romans 12	**22**	Jeremiah 51	Psalms 30
1 Samuel 15	Romans 13	**23**	Jeremiah 52	Psalms 31
1 Samuel 16	Romans 14	**24**	Lament. 1	Psalms 32
1 Samuel 17	Romans 15	**25**	Lament. 2	Psalms 33
1 Samuel 18	Romans 16	**26**	Lament. 3	Psalms 34
1 Samuel 19	1 Cor. 1	**27**	Lament. 4	Psalms 35
1 Samuel 20	1 Cor. 2	**28**	Lament. 5	Psalms 36
1 Sam. 21-22	1 Cor. 3	**29**	Ezekiel 1	Psalms 37
1 Samuel 23	1 Cor. 4	**30**	Ezekiel 2	Psalms 38
1 Samuel 24	1 Cor. 5	**31**	Ezekiel 3	Psalms 39

Abbreviations: Jer. – Jeremiah; Lament. – Lamentations;
1 Cor. – 1 Corinthians; 1 Sam. – 1 Samuel

SEPTEMBER

THE LAW OF THE LORD IS PERFECT, CONVERTING THE SOUL.

FAMILY			SECRET	
1 Samuel 25	1 Cor. 6	**1**	Ezekiel 4	Psalms 40-41
1 Samuel 26	1 Cor. 7	**2**	Ezekiel 5	Psalms 42-43
1 Samuel 27	1 Cor. 8	**3**	Ezekiel 6	Psalms 44
1 Samuel 28	1 Cor. 9	**4**	Ezekiel 7	Psalms 45
1 Sam. 29-30	1 Cor. 10	**5**	Ezekiel 8	Psalms 46-47
1 Samuel 31	1 Cor. 11	**6**	Ezekiel 9	Psalms 48
2 Samuel 1	1 Cor. 12	**7**	Ezekiel 10	Psalms 49
2 Samuel 2	1 Cor. 13	**8**	Ezekiel 11	Psalms 50
2 Samuel 3	1 Cor. 14	**9**	Ezekiel 12	Psalms 51
2 Samuel 4-5	1 Cor. 15	**10**	Ezekiel 13	Psalms 52-54
2 Samuel 6	1 Cor. 16	**11**	Ezekiel 14	Psalms 55
2 Samuel 7	2 Cor. 1	**12**	Ezekiel 15	Psalms 56-57
2 Samuel 8-9	2 Cor. 2	**13**	Ezekiel 16	Psalms 58-59
2 Samuel 10	2 Cor. 3	**14**	Ezekiel 17	Psalms 60-61
2 Samuel 11	2 Cor. 4	**15**	Ezekiel 18	Psalms 62-63
2 Samuel 12	2 Cor. 5	**16**	Ezekiel 19	Psalms 64-65
2 Samuel 13	2 Cor. 6	**17**	Ezekiel 20	Psalms 66-67
2 Samuel 14	2 Cor. 7	**18**	Ezekiel 21	Psalms 68
2 Samuel 15	2 Cor. 8	**19**	Ezekiel 22	Psalms 69
2 Samuel 16	2 Cor. 9	**20**	Ezekiel 23	Psalms 70-71
2 Samuel 17	2 Cor. 10	**21**	Ezekiel 24	Psalms 72
2 Samuel 18	2 Cor. 11	**22**	Ezekiel 25	Psalms 73
2 Samuel 19	2 Cor. 12	**23**	Ezekiel 26	Psalms 74
2 Samuel 20	2 Cor. 13	**24**	Ezekiel 27	Psalms 75-76
2 Samuel 21	Galatians 1	**25**	Ezekiel 28	Psalms 77
2 Samuel 22	Galatians 2	**26**	Ezekiel 29	Psalms 78:1-37
2 Samuel 23	Galatians 3	**27**	Ezekiel 30	Psalms 78:38
2 Samuel 24	Galatians 4	**28**	Ezekiel 31	Psalms 79
1 Kings 1	Galatians 5	**29**	Ezekiel 32	Psalms 80
1 Kings 2	Galatians 6	**30**	Ezekiel 33	Psalms 81-82

Abbreviations: 1 Cor. – 1 Corinthians; 2 Cor. – 2 Corinthians;
1 Sam. – 1 Samuel

OCTOBER

O HOW LOVE I THY LAW! IT IS MY MEDITATION ALL THE DAY.

FAMILY			SECRET	
1 Kings 3	Ephesians 1	**1**	Ezekiel 34	Psalms 83-84
1 Kings 4-5	Ephesians 2	**2**	Ezekiel 35	Psalms 85
1 Kings 6	Ephesians 3	**3**	Ezekiel 36	Psalms 86
1 Kings 7	Ephesians 4	**4**	Ezekiel 37	Psalm 87-88
1 Kings 8	Ephesians 5	**5**	Ezekiel 38	Psalms 89
1 Kings 9	Ephesians 6	**6**	Ezekiel 39	Psalms 90
1 Kings 10	Phil. 1	**7**	Ezekiel 40	Psalms 91
1 Kings 11	Phil. 2	**8**	Ezekiel 41	Ps. 92-93
1 Kings 12	Phil. 3	**9**	Ezekiel 42	Psalms 94
1 Kings 13	Phil. 4	**10**	Ezekiel 43	Ps. 95-96
1 Kings 14	Colossians 1	**11**	Ezekiel 44	Ps. 97-98
1 Kings 15	Colossians 2	**12**	Ezekiel 45	Ps. 99-101
1 Kings 16	Colossians 3	**13**	Ezekiel 46	Psalms 102
1 Kings 17	Colossians 4	**14**	Ezekiel 47	Psalms 103
1 Kings 18	1 Thess. 1	**15**	Ezekiel 48	Psalms 104
1 Kings 19	1 Thess. 2	**16**	Daniel 1	Psalms 105
1 Kings 20	1 Thess. 3	**17**	Daniel 2	Psalms 106
1 Kings 21	1 Thess. 4	**18**	Daniel 3	Psalms 107
1 Kings 22	1 Thess. 5	**19**	Daniel 4	Ps. 108-109
2 Kings 1	2 Thess. 1	**20**	Daniel 5	Ps. 110-111
2 Kings 2	2 Thess. 2	**21**	Daniel 6	Ps. 112-113
2 Kings 3	2 Thess. 3	**22**	Daniel 7	Ps. 114-115
2 Kings 4	1 Timothy 1	**23**	Daniel 8	Psalms 116
2 Kings 5	1 Timothy 2	**24**	Daniel 9	Ps. 117-118
2 Kings 6	1 Timothy 3	**25**	Daniel 10	Ps. 119:1-24
2 Kings 7	1 Timothy 4	**26**	Daniel 11	Ps. 119:25-48
2 Kings 8	1 Timothy 5	**27**	Daniel 12	Ps. 119:49-72
2 Kings 9	1 Timothy 6	**28**	Hosea 1	Ps. 119:73-96
2 Kings 10	2 Timothy 1	**29**	Hosea 2	Ps. 119:97-120
2 Kings 11-12	2 Timothy 2	**30**	Hosea 3-4	Ps. 119:121-144
2 Kings 13	2 Timothy 3	**31**	Hosea 5-6	Ps. 119:145-176

Abbreviations: Phil. – Philippians; Ps. – Psalms; 1 Thess. – 1 Thessalonians; 2 Thess. – 2 Thessalonians

NOVEMBER

AS NEWBORN BABES, DESIRE THE SINCERE MILK OF THE WORD, THAT YE MAY GROW THEREBY.

FAMILY			SECRET	
2 Kings 14	2 Timothy 4	**1**	Hosea 7	Ps. 120-122
2 Kings 15	Titus 1	**2**	Hosea 8	Ps. 123-125
2 Kings 16	Titus 2	**3**	Hosea 9	Ps. 126-128
2 Kings 17	Titus 3	**4**	Hosea 10	Ps. 129-131
2 Kings 18	Philemon	**5**	Hosea 11	Ps. 132-134
2 Kings 19	Hebrews 1	**6**	Hosea 12	Ps. 135-136
2 Kings 20	Hebrews 2	**7**	Hosea 13	Ps. 137-138
2 Kings 21	Hebrews 3	**8**	Hosea 14	Psalms 139
2 Kings 22	Hebrews 4	**9**	Joel 1	Ps. 140-141
2 Kings 23	Hebrews 5	**10**	Joel 2	Psalms 142
2 Kings 24	Hebrews 6	**11**	Joel 3	Psalms 143
2 Kings 25	Hebrews 7	**12**	Amos 1	Psalms 144
1 Chron. 1-2	Hebrews 8	**13**	Amos 2	Psalms 145
1 Chron. 3-4	Hebrews 9	**14**	Amos 3	Ps. 146-147
1 Chron. 5-6	Hebrews 10	**15**	Amos 4	Ps. 148-150
1 Chron. 7-8	Hebrews 11	**16**	Amos 5	Luke 1:1-38
1 Chron. 9-10	Hebrews 12	**17**	Amos 6	Luke 1:39
1 Chron. 11-12	Hebrews 13	**18**	Amos 7	Luke 2
1 Chron. 13-14	James 1	**19**	Amos 8	Luke 3
1 Chron. 15	James 2	**20**	Amos 9	Luke 4
1 Chron. 16	James 3	**21**	Obadiah	Luke 5
1 Chron. 17	James 4	**22**	Jonah 1	Luke 6
1 Chron. 18	James 5	**23**	Jonah 2	Luke 7
1 Chron. 19-20	1 Peter 1	**24**	Jonah 3	Luke 8
1 Chron. 21	1 Peter 2	**25**	Jonah 4	Luke 9
1 Chron. 22	1 Peter 3	**26**	Micah 1	Luke 10
1 Chron. 23	1 Peter 4	**27**	Micah 2	Luke 11
1 Chron. 24-25	1 Peter 5	**28**	Micah 3	Luke 12
1 Chron. 26-27	2 Peter 1	**29**	Micah 4	Luke 13
1 Chron. 28	2 Peter 2	**30**	Micah 5	Luke 14

Abbreviations: Ps. – Psalms; 1 Chron. – 1 Chronicles

DECEMBER

THE LAW OF HIS GOD IS IN HIS HEART; NONE OF HIS STEPS SHALL SLIDE.

FAMILY			SECRET	
1 Chron. 29	2 Peter 3	**1**	Micah 6	Luke 15
2 Chron. 1	1 John 1	**2**	Micah 7	Luke 16
2 Chron. 2	1 John 2	**3**	Nahum 1	Luke 17
2 Chron. 3-4	1 John 3	**4**	Nahum 2	Luke 18
2 Chron. 5-6:11	1 John 4	**5**	Nahum 3	Luke 19
2 Chron. 6:12	1 John 5	**6**	Hab. 1	Luke 20
2 Chron. 7	2 John	**7**	Hab. 2	Luke 21
2 Chron. 8	3 John	**8**	Hab. 3	Luke 22
2 Chron. 9	Jude	**9**	Zephaniah 1	Luke 23
2 Chron. 10	Revelation 1	**10**	Zephaniah 2	Luke 24
2 Chron. 11-12	Revelation 2	**11**	Zephaniah 3	John 1
2 Chron. 13	Revelation 3	**12**	Haggai 1	John 2
2 Chron. 14-15	Revelation 4	**13**	Haggai 2	John 3
2 Chron. 16	Revelation 5	**14**	Zechariah 1	John 4
2 Chron. 17	Revelation 6	**15**	Zechariah 2	John 5
2 Chron. 18	Revelation 7	**16**	Zechariah 3	John 6
2 Chron. 19-20	Revelation 8	**17**	Zechariah 4	John 7
2 Chron. 21	Revelation 9	**18**	Zechariah 5	John 8
2 Chron. 22-23	Rev. 10	**19**	Zechariah 6	John 9
2 Chron.24	Rev. 11	**20**	Zechariah 7	John 10
2 Chron. 25	Rev. 12	**21**	Zechariah 8	John 11
2 Chron. 26	Rev. 13	**22**	Zechariah 9	John 12
2 Chron. 27-28	Rev. 14	**23**	Zechariah 10	John 13
2 Chron. 29	Rev. 15	**24**	Zechariah 11	John 14
2 Chron. 30	Rev. 16	**25**	Zechariah 12	John 15
2 Chron. 31	Rev. 17	**26**	Zechariah 13	John 16
2 Chron. 32	Rev. 18	**27**	Zechariah 14	John 17
2 Chron. 33	Rev. 19	**28**	Malachi 1	John 18
2 Chron. 34	Rev. 20	**29**	Malachi 2	John 19
2 Chron. 35	Rev. 21	**30**	Malachi 3	John 20
2 Chron. 36	Rev. 22	**31**	Malachi 4	John 21

Abbreviations: 1 Chron. – 1 Chronicles; 2 Chron. – 2 Chronicles; Hab. – Habakkuk; Rev. – Revelation

1742 Philadelphia Baptist Confession Introduction and Instruction

THE 1742 PHILADELPHIA BAPTIST CONFESSION came forth on July 25, 1742 from a meeting held in Philadelphia by the ministers and brethren of the Baptist Association in the American colonies. Benjamin Franklin published the first edition of this first American Baptist Confession of Faith. Although this earliest of American confessions included two additional chapters, viz., "The Imposition, or Laying On of Hands" and "The Singing of Psalms in Public Worship," it was identical to its British counterpart, the 1689 London Baptist Confession; the additional chapters notwithstanding. The initial publication, and many subsequent publications of the confession, contained the introduction from the 1689 London Confession, as well as the names of the London confession participants.

This confession is an excellent systematic theology. In other words, it presents an excellent systematic explanation of the things we believe concerning God. What Charles Haddon Spurgeon had stated concerning the 1689 London Baptist Confession, a creed that defined his basic beliefs and that of his congregation at the Metropolitan Tabernacle, would just be as appropriate for the 1742 Philadelphia Confession of Faith as well:

"This ancient document is the most excellent epitome of the things most surely believed among us. It is not issued as an authoritative rule or code of faith, whereby you may be fettered, but as a means of edification in righteousness. It is an excellent, though not inspired, expression of the teaching of those Holy Scriptures by which all confessions are to be measured. We hold to the humbling truths of God's sovereign grace in the salvation of lost sinners. Salvation is through Christ alone and by faith alone."

Even if you, your family, or the church you attend as a member, have a different confession of faith than the 1742 Philadelphia Baptist Confession, I believe that you will still benefit greatly from the use of this confession and its Scripture proofs. The church I presently pastor, Sovereign Grace Baptist Church, in Anniston, Alabama, was formed as a local Baptist Church standing in agreement with the 1646 London Baptist Confession, and also in general agreement with the first American Baptist Confession called the Philadelphia Baptist Confession of 1742. I have personally held to the 1689 London Baptist Confession and have taught it to my family in our devotions; yet, I stand in agreement with our congregation in their agreement to those confessions; and the congregation, also, though it is not written as any creed within their constitution, have no objections to my stance in using the second London Baptist Confession as a defining creed. Why? Because the confessions are identical with the exception of the two additions found in the Philadelphia confession.

So how can we incorporate the 1742 Philadelphia Baptist Confession into the family devotion for the mutual edification of its members?

First, it could be read in the evenings, prior to, or after the family Bible reading from the Daily Bread Scripture portions for that day; just as the catechism is read as a supplement to the devotional Scripture portions in the morning. There are thirty-four chapters in the 1742 Confession so you might want to combine the following two-chapter combinations on the day of its appropriate reading: chapters 9 and 10; chapters 22 and 23; chapters 28 and 29; or chapters 30 and 31. In February, you may want to combine chapters 24 through 26 and chapters 28 through 31 as well.

You may also decide that you would rather just read one chapter per evening until you've read through the confession together as a family once, or even several times. It is entirely up to you. In that case, you'll want to refer to the last chapter of this family devotional for some helpful suggestions.

Philadelphia Baptist Confession

1742

1. Of the Holy Scriptures

1. THE HOLY SCRIPTURE is the only sufficient, certain, and infallible rule of all saving knowledge, faith, and obedience, although the light of nature, and the works of creation and providence do so far manifest the goodness, wisdom, and power of God, as to leave men inexcusable; yet are they not sufficient to give that knowledge of God and his will which is necessary unto salvation. Therefore it pleased the Lord at sundry times and in divers manners to reveal himself, and to declare that his will unto his church; and afterward for the better preserving and propagating of the truth, and for the more sure establishment and comfort of the church against the corruption of the flesh, and the malice of Satan, and of the world, to commit the same wholly unto writing; which maketh the Holy Scriptures to be most necessary, those former ways of God's revealing his will unto his people being now ceased.[1]

2. UNDER THE NAME of Holy Scripture, or the Word of God written, are now contained all the books of the Old and New

Testaments, which are these:

> **Of the Old Testament:** Genesis, Exodus, Leviticus, Numbers, Deuteronomy, Joshua, Judges, Ruth, 1 Samuel, 2 Samuel, 1 Kings, 2 Kings, 1 Chronicles, 2 Chronicles, Ezra, Nehemiah, Esther, Job, Psalms, Proverbs, Ecclesiastes, Song of Solomon, Isaiah, Jeremiah, Lamentations, Ezekiel, Daniel, Hosea, Joel, Amos, Obadiah, Jonah, Micah, Nahum, Habakkuk, Zephaniah, Haggai, Zechariah, Malachi
>
> **Of the New Testament:** Matthew, Mark, Luke, John, Acts, Romans, 1 Corinthians, 2 Corinthians, Galatians, Ephesians, Philippians, Colossians, 1 Thessalonians, 2 Thessalonians, 1 Timothy, 2 Timothy, Titus, Philemon, Hebrews, James, 1 Peter, 2 Peter, 1 John, 2 John, 3 John, Jude, Revelation

All of these books are given by the inspiration of God to be the standard of faith and life.[2]

3. The books commonly called Apocrypha, not being of divine inspiration, are no part of the canon or rule of the Scripture, and, therefore, are of no authority to the church of God, nor to be any otherwise approved or made use of than other human writings.[3]

4. The authority of the Holy Scripture, for which it ought to be believed, dependeth not upon the testimony of any man or church, but wholly upon God (who is truth itself), the author thereof; therefore it is to be received because it is the Word of God.[4]

5. We may be moved and induced by the testimony of the church of God to an high and reverent esteem of the Holy Scriptures; and the heavenliness of the matter, the efficacy of the doctrine, and the majesty of the style, the consent of all the parts, the scope of the whole (which is to give all glory to God), the full discovery it makes of the only way of man's salvation, and many

other incomparable excellencies, and entire perfections thereof, are arguments whereby it doth abundantly evidence itself to be the Word of God; yet notwithstanding, our full persuasion and assurance of the infallible truth, and divine authority thereof, is from the inward work of the Holy Spirit bearing witness by and with the Word in our hearts.[5]

6. THE WHOLE COUNSEL OF GOD concerning all things necessary for his own glory, man's salvation, faith and life, is either expressly set down or necessarily contained in the Holy Scripture: unto which nothing at any time is to be added, whether by new revelation of the Spirit, or traditions of men. Nevertheless, we acknowledge the inward illumination of the Spirit of God to be necessary for the saving understanding of such things as are revealed in the Word, and that there are some circumstances concerning the worship of God, and government of the church, common to human actions and societies, which are to be ordered by the light of nature and Christian prudence, according to the general rules of the Word, which are always to be observed.[6]

7. ALL THINGS IN SCRIPTURE are not alike plain in themselves, nor alike clear unto all; yet those things which are necessary to be known, believed and observed for salvation, are so clearly propounded and opened in some place of Scripture or other, that not only the learned, but the unlearned, in a due use of ordinary means, may attain to a sufficient understanding of them.[7]

8. THE OLD TESTAMENT in Hebrew (which was the native language of the people of God of old), and the New Testament in Greek (which at the time of the writing of it was most generally known to the nations), being immediately inspired by God, and by his singular care and providence kept pure in all ages, are therefore authentic; so as in all controversies of religion, the church is finally to appeal to them. But because these original tongues are not known to all the people of God, who have a right unto, and interest in the Scriptures, and are commanded in the fear of God to read and search them, therefore they are to be translated into the vulgar language of every nation unto which they come, that the Word of God dwelling plentifully in all, they

may worship him in an acceptable manner, and through patience and comfort of the Scriptures may have hope.[8]

9. THE INFALLIBLE RULE of interpretation of Scripture is the Scripture itself; and therefore when there is a question about the true and full sense of any Scripture (which is not manifold, but one), it must be searched by other places that speak more clearly.[9]

10. THE SUPREME JUDGE, BY which all controversies of religion are to be determined, and all decrees of councils, opinions of ancient writers, doctrines of men, and private spirits, are to be examined, and in whose sentence we are to rest, can be no other but the Holy Scripture delivered by the Spirit, into which Scripture so delivered, our faith is finally resolved.[10]

2. Of God and the Holy Trinity

1. THE LORD OUR GOD is but one only living and true God; whose subsistence is in and of himself, infinite in being and perfection; whose essence cannot be comprehended by any but himself; a most pure spirit, invisible, without body, parts, or passions, who only hath immortality, dwelling in the light which no man can approach unto; who is immutable, immense, eternal, incomprehensible, almighty, every way infinite, most holy, most wise, most free, most absolute; working all things according to the counsel of his own immutable and most righteous will for his own glory; most loving, gracious, merciful, long-suffering, abundant in goodness and truth, forgiving iniquity, transgression, and sin; the rewarder of them that diligently seek him, and withal most just and terrible in his judgments, hating all sin, and who will by no means clear the guilty.[11]

2. GOD, HAVING ALL LIFE, glory, goodness, blessedness, in and of himself, is alone in and unto himself all-sufficient, not standing in need of any creature which he hath made, nor deriving any glory from them, but only manifesting his own glory in, by, unto, and upon them; he is the alone fountain of all being, of whom, through whom, and to whom are all things, and he hath most sovereign dominion over all creatures, to do by them, for

them, or upon them, whatsoever himself pleaseth; in his sight all things are open and manifest, his knowledge is infinite, infallible, and independent upon the creature, so as nothing is to him contingent or uncertain; he is most holy in all his counsels, in all his works, and in all his commands; to him is due from angels and men, whatsoever worship, service, or obedience, as creatures they owe unto the Creator, and whatever he is further pleased to require of them.[12]

3. IN THIS DIVINE and infinite Being there are three subsistences, the Father, the Word (or Son), and Holy Spirit, of one substance, power, and eternity, each having the whole divine essence, yet the essence undivided: the Father is of none, neither begotten nor proceeding; the Son is eternally begotten of the Father; the Holy Spirit proceeding from the Father and the Son; all infinite, without beginning, therefore but one God, who is not to be divided in nature and being, but distinguished by several peculiar relative properties and personal relations; which doctrine of the Trinity is the foundation of all our communion with God, and comfortable dependence on him.[13]

3. Of God's Decree

1. GOD HATH DECREED IN HIMSELF, from all eternity, by the most wise and holy counsel of his own will, freely and unchangeably, all things, whatsoever comes to pass; yet so as thereby is God neither the author of sin nor hath fellowship with any therein; nor is violence offered to the will of the creature, nor yet is the liberty or contingency of second causes taken away, but rather established; in which appears his wisdom in disposing all things, and power and faithfulness in accomplishing his decree.[14]

2. ALTHOUGH GOD KNOWETH whatsoever may or can come to pass, upon all supposed conditions, yet hath he not decreed anything, because he foresaw it as future, or as that which would come to pass upon such conditions.[15]

3. BY THE DECREE OF GOD, for the manifestation of his glory, some men and angels are predestinated, or foreordained to eternal

life through Jesus Christ, to the praise of his glorious grace; others being left to act in their sin to their just condemnation, to the praise of his glorious justice.[16]

4. THESE ANGELS and men thus predestinated and foreordained, are particularly and unchangeably designed, and their number so certain and definite, that it cannot be either increased or diminished.[17]

5. THOSE OF MANKIND that are predestinated to life, God, before the foundation of the world was laid, according to his eternal and immutable purpose, and the secret counsel and good pleasure of his will, hath chosen in Christ unto everlasting glory, out of his mere free grace and love, without any other thing in the creature as a condition or cause moving him thereunto.[18]

6. AS GOD HATH APPOINTED the elect unto glory, so he hath, by the eternal and most free purpose of his will, foreordained all the means thereunto; wherefore they who are elected, being fallen in Adam, are redeemed by Christ, are effectually called unto faith in Christ, by his Spirit working in due season, are justified, adopted, sanctified, and kept by his power through faith unto salvation; neither are any other redeemed by Christ, or effectually called, justified, adopted, sanctified, and saved, but the elect only.[19]

7. THE DOCTRINE of the high mystery of predestination is to be handled with special prudence and care, that men attending the will of God revealed in his Word, and yielding obedience thereunto, may, from the certainty of their effectual vocation, be assured of their eternal election; so shall this doctrine afford matter of praise, reverence, and admiration of God, and of humility, diligence, and abundant consolation to all that sincerely obey the gospel.[20]

4. Of Creation

1. IN THE BEGINNING it pleased God the Father, Son, and Holy Spirit, for the manifestation of the glory of his eternal power, wisdom, and goodness, to create or make the world, and all things

therein, whether visible or invisible, in the space of six days, and all very good.[21]

2. AFTER GOD had made all other creatures, he created man, male and female, with reasonable and immortal souls, rendering them fit unto that life to God for which they were created; being made after the image of God, in knowledge, righteousness, and true holiness; having the law of God written in their hearts, and power to fulfil it, and yet under a possibility of transgressing, being left to the liberty of their own will, which was subject to change.[22]

3. BESIDES THE LAW written in their hearts, they received a command not to eat of the tree of knowledge of good and evil, which whilst they kept, they were happy in their communion with God, and had dominion over the creatures.[23]

5. Of Divine Providence

1. GOD THE GOOD CREATOR OF ALL THINGS, in his infinite power and wisdom doth uphold, direct, dispose, and govern all creatures and things, from the greatest even to the least, by his most wise and holy providence, to the end for the which they were created, according unto his infallible foreknowledge, and the free and immutable counsel of his own will; to the praise of the glory of his wisdom, power, justice, infinite goodness, and mercy.[24]

2. ALTHOUGH in relation to the foreknowledge and decree of God, the first cause, all things come to pass immutably and infallibly; so that there is not anything befalls any by chance, or without his providence; yet by the same providence he ordereth them to fall out according to the nature of second causes, either necessarily, freely, or contingently.[25]

3. GOD, IN HIS ORDINARY PROVIDENCE maketh use of means, yet is free to work without, above, and against them at his pleasure.[26]

4. THE ALMIGHTY POWER, unsearchable wisdom, and infinite goodness of God, so far manifest themselves in his providence,

that his determinate counsel extendeth itself even to the first fall, and all other sinful actions both of angels and men; and that not by a bare permission, which also he most wisely and powerfully boundeth, and otherwise ordereth and governeth, in a manifold dispensation to his most holy ends; yet so, as the sinfulness of their acts proceedeth only from the creatures, and not from God, who, being most holy and righteous, neither is nor can be the author or approver of sin.[27]

5. THE MOST WISE, righteous, and gracious God doth oftentimes leave for a season his own children to manifold temptations and the corruptions of their own hearts, to chastise them for their former sins, or to discover unto them the hidden strength of corruption and deceitfulness of their hearts, that they may be humbled; and to raise them to a more close and constant dependence for their support upon himself; and to make them more watchful against all future occasions of sin, and for other just and holy ends. So that whatsoever befalls any of his elect is by his appointment, for his glory, and their good.[28]

6. AS FOR THOSE WICKED and ungodly men whom God, as the righteous judge, for former sin doth blind and harden; from them he not only withholdeth his grace, whereby they might have been enlightened in their understanding, and wrought upon their hearts; but sometimes also withdraweth the gifts which they had, and exposeth them to such objects as their corruption makes occasion of sin; and withal, gives them over to their own lusts, the temptations of the world, and the power of Satan, whereby it comes to pass that they harden themselves, under those means which God useth for the softening of others.[29]

7. AS THE PROVIDENCE OF GOD doth in general reach to all creatures, so after a more special manner it taketh care of his church, and disposeth of all things to the good thereof.[30]

6. Of the Fall of Man, Sin, and Punishment

1. ALTHOUGH GOD CREATED MAN UPRIGHT and perfect, and gave him a righteous law, which had been unto life had he kept it,

and threatened death upon the breach thereof, yet he did not long abide in this honour; Satan using the subtlety of the serpent to subdue Eve, then by her seducing Adam, who, without any compulsion, did willfully transgress the law of their creation, and the command given unto them, in eating the forbidden fruit, which God was pleased, according to his wise and holy counsel to permit, having purposed to order it to his own glory.[31]

2. OUR FIRST PARENTS, by this sin, fell from their original righteousness and communion with God, and we in them whereby death came upon all: all becoming dead in sin, and wholly defiled in all the faculties and parts of soul and body.[32]

3. THEY BEING THE ROOT, and by God's appointment, standing in the room and stead of all mankind, the guilt of the sin was imputed, and corrupted nature conveyed, to all their posterity descending from them by ordinary generation, being now conceived in sin, and by nature children of wrath, the servants of sin, the subjects of death, and all other miseries, spiritual, temporal, and eternal, unless the Lord Jesus set them free.[33]

4. FROM THIS ORIGINAL CORRUPTION, whereby we are utterly indisposed, disabled, and made opposite to all good, and wholly inclined to all evil, do proceed all actual transgressions.[34]

5. The corruption of nature, during this life, doth remain in those that are regenerated; and although it be through Christ pardoned and mortified, yet both itself, and the first motions thereof, are truly and properly sin.[35]

7. Of God's Covenant

1. THE DISTANCE BETWEEN GOD and the creature is so great, that although reasonable creatures do owe obedience to him as their creator, yet they could never have attained the reward of life but by some voluntary condescension on God's part, which he hath been pleased to express by way of covenant.[36]

2. MOREOVER, man having brought himself under the curse of the law by his fall, it pleased the Lord to make a covenant of

grace, wherein he freely offereth unto sinners life and salvation by Jesus Christ, requiring of them faith in him, that they may be saved; and promising to give unto all those that are ordained unto eternal life, his Holy Spirit, to make them willing and able to believe.[37]

3. THIS COVENANT is revealed in the gospel; first of all to Adam in the promise of salvation by the seed of the woman, and afterwards by farther steps, until the full discovery thereof was completed in the New Testament; and it is founded in that eternal covenant transaction that was between the Father and the Son about the redemption of the elect; and it is alone by the grace of this covenant that all the posterity of fallen Adam that ever were saved did obtain life and blessed immortality, man being now utterly incapable of acceptance with God upon those terms on which Adam stood in his state of innocency.[38]

8. Of Christ the Mediator

1. IT PLEASED GOD, in his eternal purpose, to choose and ordain the Lord Jesus, his only begotten Son, according to the covenant made between them both, to be the mediator between God and man; the prophet, priest, and king; head and saviour of the church, the heir of all things, and judge of the world; unto whom he did from all eternity give a people to be his seed and to be by him in time redeemed, called, justified, sanctified, and glorified.[39]

2. THE SON OF GOD, the second person in the Holy Trinity, being very and eternal God, the brightness of the Father's glory, of one substance and equal with him who made the world, who upholdeth and governeth all things he hath made, did, when the fullness of time was come, take upon him man's nature, with all the essential properties and common infirmities thereof, yet without sin; being conceived by the Holy Spirit in the womb of the Virgin Mary, the Holy Spirit coming down upon her: and the power of the Most High overshadowing her; and so was made of a woman of the tribe of Judah, of the seed of Abraham and David

according to the Scriptures; so that two whole, perfect, and distinct natures were inseparably joined together in one person, without conversion, composition, or confusion; which person is very God and very man, yet one Christ, the only mediator between God and man.[40]

3. THE LORD JESUS, in his human nature thus united to the divine, in the person of the Son, was sanctified and anointed with the Holy Spirit above measure, having in him all the treasures of wisdom and knowledge; in whom it pleased the Father that all fullness should dwell, to the end that being holy, harmless, undefiled, and full of grace and truth, he might be throughly furnished to execute the office of mediator and surety; which office he took not upon himself, but was thereunto called by his Father; who also put all power and judgment in his hand, and gave him commandment to execute the same.[41]

4. THIS OFFICE the Lord Jesus did most willingly undertake, which that he might discharge he was made under the law, and did perfectly fulfil it, and underwent the punishment due to us, which we should have borne and suffered, being made sin and a curse for us; enduring most grievous sorrows in his soul, and most painful sufferings in his body; was crucified, and died, and remained in the state of the dead, yet saw no corruption: on the third day he arose from the dead with the same body in which he suffered, with which he also ascended into heaven, and there sitteth at the right hand of his Father making intercession, and shall return to judge men and angels at the end of the world.[42]

5. THE LORD JESUS, by his perfect obedience and sacrifice of himself, which he through the eternal Spirit once offered up unto God, hath fully satisfied the justice of God, procured reconciliation, and purchased an everlasting inheritance in the kingdom of heaven, for all those whom the Father hath given unto him.[43]

6. ALTHOUGH the price of redemption was not actually paid by Christ till after his incarnation, yet the virtue, efficacy, and benefit thereof were communicated to the elect in all ages, successively from the beginning of the world, in and by those

promises, types, and sacrifices wherein he was revealed, and signified to be the seed which should bruise the serpent's head; and the Lamb slain from the foundation of the world, being the same yesterday, and today and for ever.[44]

7. CHRIST, in the work of mediation, acteth according to both natures, by each nature doing that which is proper to itself; yet by reason of the unity of the person, that which is proper to one nature is sometimes in Scripture, attributed to the person denominated by the other nature.[45]

8. TO ALL THOSE for whom Christ hath obtained eternal redemption, he doth certainly and effectually apply and communicate the same, making intercession for them; uniting them to himself by his Spirit, revealing unto them, in and by his Word, the mystery of salvation, persuading them to believe and obey, governing their hearts by his Word and Spirit, and overcoming all their enemies by his almighty power and wisdom, in such manner and ways as are most consonant to his wonderful and unsearchable dispensation; and all of free and absolute grace, without any condition foreseen in them to procure it.[46]

9. THIS OFFICE of mediator between God and man is proper only to Christ, who is the prophet, priest, and king of the church of God; and may not be either in whole, or any part thereof, transferred from him to any other.[47]

10. This number and order of offices is necessary; for in respect of our ignorance, we stand in need of his prophetical office; and in respect of our alienation from God, and imperfection of the best of our services, we need his priestly office to reconcile us and present us acceptable unto God; and in respect to our averseness and utter inability to return to God, and for our rescue and security from our spiritual adversaries, we need his kingly office to convince, subdue, draw, uphold, deliver, and preserve us to his heavenly kingdom.[48]

9. Of Free Will

1. GOD HATH ENDUED the will of man with that natural

liberty and power of acting upon choice, that it is neither forced, nor by any necessity of nature determined to do good or evil.[49]

2. MAN, in his state of innocency, had freedom and power to will and to do that which was good and well-pleasing to God, but yet was unstable, so that he might fall from it.[50]

3. MAN, by his fall into a state of sin, hath wholly lost all ability of will to any spiritual good accompanying salvation; so as a natural man, being altogether averse from that good, and dead in sin, is not able by his own strength to convert himself, or to prepare himself thereunto.[51]

4. WHEN GOD converts a sinner, and translates him into the state of grace, he freeth him from his natural bondage under sin, and by his grace alone enables him freely to will and to do that which is spiritually good; yet so as that by reason of his remaining corruptions, he doth not perfectly, nor only will, that which is good, but doth also will that which is evil.[52]

5. THIS WILL OF MAN is made perfectly and immutably free to good alone in the state of glory only.[53]

10. Of Effectual Calling

1. THOSE WHOM GOD hath predestinated unto life, he is pleased in his appointed, and accepted time, effectually to call, by his Word and Spirit, out of that state of sin and death in which they are by nature, to grace and salvation by Jesus Christ; enlightening their minds spiritually and savingly to understand the things of God; taking away their heart of stone, and giving unto them a heart of flesh; renewing their wills, and by his almighty power determining them to that which is good, and effectually drawing them to Jesus Christ; yet so as they come most freely, being made willing by his grace.[54]

2. THIS EFFECTUAL CALL is of God's free and special grace alone, not from anything at all foreseen in man, nor from any power or agency in the creature, being wholly passive therein, being dead in sins and trespasses, until being quickened and renewed by the Holy Spirit; he is thereby enabled to answer this

call, and to embrace the grace offered and conveyed in it, and that by no less power than that which raised up Christ from the dead.[55]

3. ELECT INFANTS dying in infancy are regenerated and saved by Christ through the Spirit; who worketh when, and where, and how he pleases; so also are all elect persons, who are incapable of being outwardly called by the ministry of the Word.[56]

4. OTHERS NOT ELECTED, although they may be called by the ministry of the Word, and may have some common operations of the Spirit, yet not being effectually drawn by the Father, they neither will nor can truly come to Christ, and therefore cannot be saved: much less can men that receive not the Christian religion be saved; be they never so diligent to frame their lives according to the light of nature and the law of that religion they do profess.[57]

11. Of Justification

1. THOSE WHOM GOD effectually calleth, he also freely justifieth, not by infusing righteousness into them, but by pardoning their sins, and by accounting and accepting their persons as righteous; not for anything wrought in them, or done by them, but for Christ's sake alone; not by imputing faith itself, the act of believing, or any other evangelical obedience to them, as their righteousness; but by imputing Christ's active obedience unto the whole law, and passive obedience in his death for their whole and sole righteousness by faith, which faith they have not of themselves; it is the gift of God.[58]

2. FAITH thus receiving and resting on Christ and his righteousness, is the alone instrument of justification; yet it is not alone in the person justified, but is ever accompanied with all other saving graces, and is no dead faith, but worketh by love.[59]

3. CHRIST, by His obedience and death, did fully discharge the debt of all those that are justified; and did, by the sacrifice of Himself in the blood of his cross, undergoing in their stead the penalty due unto them, make a proper, real, and full satisfaction to God's justice in their behalf; yet, inasmuch as he was given by the Father for them, and his obedience and satisfaction accepted in

their stead, and both freely, not for anything in them, their justification is only of free grace, that both the exact justice and rich grace of God might be glorified in the justification of sinners.[60]

4. GOD did from all eternity decree to justify all the elect, and Christ did in the fullness of time die for their sins, and rise again for their justification; nevertheless, they are not justified personally, until the Holy Spirit doth in time due actually apply Christ unto them.[61]

5. GOD doth continue to forgive the sins of those that are justified, and although they can never fall from the state of justification, yet they may, by their sins, fall under God's fatherly displeasure; and in that condition they have not usually the light of his countenance restored unto them, until they humble themselves, confess their sins, beg pardon, and renew their faith and repentance.[62]

6. THE JUSTIFICATION of believers under the Old Testament was, in all these respects, one and the same with the justification of believers under the New Testament.[63]

12. Of Adoption

ALL THOSE that are justified, God vouchsafed, in and for the sake of his only Son Jesus Christ, to make partakers of the grace of adoption, by which they are taken into the number, and enjoy the liberties and privileges of the children of God, have his name put upon them, receive the spirit of adoption, have access to the throne of grace with boldness, are enabled to cry Abba, Father, are pitied, protected, provided for, and chastened by him as by a Father, yet never cast off, but sealed to the day of redemption, and inherit the promises as heirs of everlasting salvation.[64]

13. Of Sanctification

1. THEY WHO ARE united to Christ, effectually called, and regenerated, having a new heart and a new spirit created in them

through the virtue of Christ's death and resurrection, are also farther sanctified, really and personally, through the same virtue, by his Word and Spirit dwelling in them; the dominion of the whole body of sin is destroyed, and the several lusts thereof are more and more weakened and mortified, and they more and more quickened and strengthened in all saving graces, to the practice of all true holiness, without which no man shall see the Lord.[65]

2. THIS SANCTIFICATION is throughout the whole man, yet imperfect in this life; there abideth still some remnants of corruption in every part, whence ariseth a continual and irreconcilable war; the flesh lusting against the Spirit, and the Spirit against the flesh.[66]

3. IN WHICH WAR, although the remaining corruption for a time may much prevail, yet through the continual supply of strength from the sanctifying Spirit of Christ, the regenerate part doth overcome; and so the saints grow in grace, perfecting holiness in the fear of God, pressing after a heavenly life, in evangelical obedience to all the commands which Christ as Head and King, in his Word hath prescribed them.[67]

14. Of Saving Faith

1. THE GRACE OF FAITH, whereby the elect are enabled to believe to the saving of their souls, is the work of the Spirit of Christ in their hearts, and is ordinarily wrought by the ministry of the Word; by which also, and by the administration of baptism and the Lord's Supper, prayer, and other means appointed of God, it is increased and strengthened.[68]

2. BY THIS FAITH a Christian believeth to be true whatsoever is revealed in the Word for the authority of God himself, and also apprehendeth an excellency therein above all other writings and all things in the world, as it bears forth the glory of God in his attributes, the excellency of Christ in his nature and offices, and the power and fullness of the Holy Spirit in his workings and operations: and so is enabled to cast his soul upon the truth thus believed; and also acteth differently upon that which each

particular passage thereof containeth; yielding obedience to the commands, trembling at the threatenings, and embracing the promises of God for this life and that which is to come; but the principal acts of saving faith have immediate relation to Christ, accepting, receiving, and resting upon him alone for justification, sanctification, and eternal life, by virtue of the covenant of grace.[69]

3. THIS FAITH, although it be different in degrees, and may be weak or strong, yet it is in the least degree of it different in the kind or nature of it, as is all other saving grace, from the faith and common grace of temporary believers; and therefore, though it may be many times assailed and weakened, yet it gets the victory, growing up in many to the attainment of a full assurance through Christ, who is both the author and finisher of our faith.[70]

15. Of Repentance unto Life and Salvation

1. SUCH OF THE ELECT as are converted at riper years, having sometime lived in the state of nature, and therein served divers lusts and pleasures, God in their effectual calling giveth them repentance unto life.[71]

2. WHEREAS there is none that doth good and sinneth not, and the best of men may, through the power and deceitfulness of their corruption dwelling in them, with the prevalency of temptation, fall into great sins and provocations; God hath, in the covenant of grace, mercifully provided that believers so sinning and falling be renewed through repentance unto salvation.[72]

3. THIS SAVING REPENTANCE is an evangelical grace, whereby a person, being by the Holy Spirit made sensible of the manifold evils of his sin, doth, by faith in Christ, humble himself for it with godly sorrow, detestation of it, and self-abhorrency, praying for pardon and strength of grace, with a purpose and endeavor, by supplies of the Spirit, to walk before God unto all well-pleasing in all things.[73]

4. AS REPENTANCE is to be continued through the whole course of our lives, upon the account of the body of death, and the motions thereof, so it is every man's duty to repent of his

particular known sins particularly.[74]

5. SUCH IS THE PROVISION which God hath made through Christ in the covenant of grace for the preservation of believers unto salvation; that although there is no sin so small but it deserves damnation; yet there is no sin so great that it shall bring damnation on them that repent; which makes the constant preaching of repentance necessary.[75]

16. Of Good Works

1. GOOD WORKS are only such as God hath commanded in his Holy Word, and not such as without the warrant thereof are devised by men out of blind zeal, or upon any pretence of good intentions.[76]

2. THESE GOOD WORKS, done in obedience to God's commandments, are the fruits and evidences of a true and lively faith; and by them believers manifest their thankfulness, strengthen their assurance, edify their brethren, adorn the profession of the gospel, stop the mouths of the adversaries, and glorify God, whose workmanship they are, created in Christ Jesus thereunto, that having their fruit unto holiness they may have the end eternal life.[77]

3. THEIR ABILITY to do good works is not at all of themselves, but wholly from the Spirit of Christ; and that they may be enabled thereunto, besides the graces they have already received, there is necessary an actual influence of the same Holy Spirit, to work in them to will and to do of his good pleasure; yet they are not hereupon to grow negligent, as if they were not bound to perform any duty, unless upon a special motion of the Spirit, but they ought to be diligent in stirring up the grace of God that is in them.[78]

4. THEY WHO in their obedience attain to the greatest height which is possible in this life, are so far from being able to supererogate, and to do more than God requires, as that they fall short of much which in duty they are bound to do.[79]

5. WE CANNOT by our best works merit pardon of sin or

eternal life at the hand of God, by reason of the great disproportion that is between them and the glory to come, and the infinite distance that is between us and God, whom by them we can neither profit nor satisfy for the debt of our former sins; but when we have done all we can, we have done but our duty, and are unprofitable servants; and because as they are good they proceed from his Spirit, and as they are wrought by us they are defiled and mixed with so much weakness and imperfection, that they cannot endure the severity of God's punishment.[80]

6. YET NOTWITHSTANDING the persons of believers being accepted through Christ, their good works also are accepted in him; not as though they were in this life wholly unblameable and unreprovable in God's sight, but that he, looking upon them in his Son, is pleased to accept and reward that which is sincere, although accompanied with many weaknesses and imperfections.[81]

7. WORKS DONE by unregenerate men, although for the matter of them they may be things which God commands, and of good use both to themselves and others; yet because they proceed not from a heart purified by faith, nor are done in a right manner according to the Word, nor to a right end, the glory of God, they are therefore sinful, and cannot please God, nor make a man meet to receive grace from God, and yet their neglect of them is more sinful and displeasing to God.[82]

17. Of the Perseverance of the Saints

1. THOSE WHOM GOD hath accepted in the beloved, effectually called and sanctified by his Spirit, and given the precious faith of his elect unto, can neither totally nor finally fall from the state of grace, but shall certainly persevere therein to the end, and be eternally saved, seeing the gifts and callings of God are without repentance, whence he still begets and nourisheth in them faith, repentance, love, joy, hope, and all the graces of the Spirit unto immortality; and though many storms and floods arise and beat against them, yet they shall never be able to take them off

that foundation and rock which by faith they are fastened upon; notwithstanding, through unbelief and the temptations of Satan, the sensible sight of the light and love of God may for a time be clouded and obscured from them, yet he is still the same, and they shall be sure to be kept by the power of God unto salvation, where they shall enjoy their purchased possession, they being engraven upon the palm of his hands, and their names having been written in the book of life from all eternity.[83]

2. THIS PERSEVERANCE of the saints depends not upon their own free will, but upon the immutability of the decree of election, flowing from the free and unchangeable love of God the Father, upon the efficacy of the merit and intercession of Jesus Christ and union with him, the oath of God, the abiding of his Spirit, and the seed of God within them, and the nature of the covenant of grace; from all which ariseth also the certainty and infallibility thereof.[84]

3. AND THOUGH they may, through the temptation of Satan and of the world, the prevalency of corruption remaining in them, and the neglect of means of their preservation, fall into grievous sins, and for a time continue therein, whereby they incur God's displeasure and grieve his Holy Spirit, come to have their graces and comforts impaired, have their hearts hardened, and their consciences wounded, hurt and scandalize others, and bring temporal judgments upon themselves, yet shall they renew their repentance and be preserved through faith in Christ Jesus to the end.[85]

18. Of Assurance of Grace and Salvation

1. ALTHOUGH TEMPORARY BELIEVERS, and other unregenerate men, may vainly deceive themselves with false hopes and carnal presumptions of being in the favor of God and state of salvation, which hope of theirs shall perish; yet such as truly believe in the Lord Jesus, and love him in sincerity, endeavoring to walk in all good conscience before him, may in this life be certainly assured that they are in the state of grace, and may rejoice in the hope of the glory of God, which hope shall never make them ashamed.[86]

2. THIS CERTAINTY is not a bare conjectural and probable persuasion grounded upon a fallible hope, but an infallible assurance of faith founded on the blood and righteousness of Christ revealed in the gospel; and also upon the inward evidence of those graces of the Spirit unto which promises are made, and on the testimony of the Spirit of adoption, witnessing with our spirits that we are the children of God; and, as a fruit thereof, keeping the heart both humble and holy.[87]

3. THIS INFALLIBLE ASSURANCE doth not so belong to the essence of faith, but that a true believer may wait long, and conflict with many difficulties before he be partaker of it; yet being enabled by the Spirit to know the things which are freely given him of God, he may, without extraordinary revelation, in the right use of means, attain thereunto: and therefore it is the duty of every one to give all diligence to make his calling and election sure, that thereby his heart may be enlarged in peace and joy in the Holy Spirit, in love and thankfulness to God, and in strength and cheerfulness in the duties of obedience, the proper fruits of this assurance; —so far is it from inclining men to looseness.[88]

4. TRUE BELIEVERS may have the assurance of their salvation diverse ways shaken, diminished, and intermitted; as by negligence in preserving of it, by falling into some special sin which woundeth the conscience and grieveth the Spirit; by some sudden or vehement temptation, by God's withdrawing the light of his countenance, and suffering even such as fear him to walk in darkness and to have no light, yet are they never destitute of the seed of God and life of faith, that love of Christ and the brethren, that sincerity of heart and conscience of duty out of which, by the operation of the Spirit, this assurance may in due time be revived, and by the which, in the meantime, they are preserved from utter despair.[89]

19. Of the Law of God

1. GOD GAVE TO ADAM a law of universal obedience written in his heart, and a particular precept of not eating the fruit of the tree of knowledge of good and evil; by which he bound him and

all his posterity to personal, entire, exact, and perpetual obedience; promised life upon the fulfilling, and threatened death upon the breach of it, and endued him with power and ability to keep it.[90]

2. THE SAME LAW that was first written in the heart of man continued to be a perfect rule of righteousness after the fall, and was delivered by God upon Mount Sinai, in ten commandments, and written in two tables, the four first containing our duty towards God, and the other six, our duty to man.[91]

3. BESIDES THIS LAW, commonly called moral, God was pleased to give to the people of Israel ceremonial laws, containing several typical ordinances, partly of worship, prefiguring Christ, his graces, actions, sufferings, and benefits; and partly holding forth divers instructions of moral duties, all which ceremonial laws being appointed only to the time of reformation, are, by Jesus Christ the true Messiah and only law-giver, who was furnished with power from the Father for that end abrogated and taken away.[92]

4. TO THEM ALSO he gave sundry judicial laws, which expired together with the state of that people, not obliging any now by virtue of that institution; their general equity only being of moral use.[93]

5. THE MORAL LAW doth for ever bind all, as well justified persons as others, to the obedience thereof, and that not only in regard of the matter contained in it, but also in respect of the authority of God the Creator, who gave it; neither doth Christ in the gospel any way dissolve, but much strengthen this obligation.[94]

6. ALTHOUGH TRUE BELIEVERS be not under the law as a covenant of works, to be thereby justified or condemned, yet it is of great use to them as well as to others, in that as a rule of life, informing them of the will of God and their duty, it directs and binds them to walk accordingly; discovering also the sinful pollutions of their natures, hearts, and lives, so as examining themselves thereby, they may come to further conviction of, humiliation for, and hatred against, sin; together with a clearer

sight of the need they have of Christ and the perfection of his obedience; it is likewise of use to the regenerate to restrain their corruptions, in that it forbids sin; and the threatenings of it serve to show what even their sins deserve, and what afflictions in this life they may expect for them, although freed from the curse and unallayed rigor thereof. The promises of it likewise show them God's approbation of obedience, and what blessings they may expect upon the performance thereof, though not as due to them by the law as a covenant of works; so as man's doing good and refraining from evil, because the law encourageth to the one and deterreth from the other, is no evidence of his being under the law and not under grace.[95]

7. NEITHER are the aforementioned uses of the law contrary to the grace of the gospel, but do sweetly comply with it, the Spirit of Christ subduing and enabling the will of man to do that freely and cheerfully which the will of God, revealed in the law, requireth to be done.[96]

20. Of the Gospel and Extent of Grace

1. THE COVENANT OF WORKS being broken by sin, and made unprofitable unto life, God was pleased to give forth the promise of Christ, the seed of the woman, as the means of calling the elect, and begetting in them faith and repentance; in this promise the gospel, as to the substance of it, was revealed, and therein effectual for the conversion and salvation of sinners.[97]

2. THIS PROMISE OF CHRIST, and salvation by him, is revealed only by the Word of God; neither do the works of creation or providence, with the light of nature, make discovery of Christ, or of grace by him, so much as in a general or obscure way; much less that men destitute of the revelation of him by the promise or gospel, should be enabled thereby to attain saving faith or repentance.[98]

3. THE REVELATION of the gospel unto sinners, made in diverse times and by sundry parts, with the addition of promises and precepts for the obedience required therein, as to the nations

and persons to whom it is granted, is merely of the sovereign will and good pleasure of God; not being annexed by virtue of any promise to the due improvement of men's natural abilities, by virtue of common light received without it, which none ever did make, or can do so; and therefore in all ages, the preaching of the gospel has been granted unto persons and nations, as to the extent or straitening of it, in great variety, according to the counsel of the will of God.[99]

4. ALTHOUGH the gospel be the only outward means of revealing Christ and saving grace, and is, as such, abundantly sufficient thereunto; yet that men who are dead in trespasses may be born again, quickened or regenerated, there is moreover necessary an effectual insuperable work of the Holy Spirit upon the whole soul, for the producing in them a new spiritual life; without which no other means will effect their conversion unto God.[100]

21. Of Christian Liberty and Liberty of Conscience

1. THE LIBERTY WHICH CHRIST hath purchased for believers under the gospel, consists in their freedom from the guilt of sin, the condemning wrath of God, the rigor and curse of the law, and in their being delivered from this present evil world, bondage to Satan, and dominion of sin, from the evil of afflictions, the fear and sting of death, the victory of the grave, and everlasting damnation: as also in their free access to God, and their yielding obedience unto him, not out of slavish fear, but a childlike love and willing mind.

ALL WHICH were common also to believers under the law for the substance of them; but under the New Testament the liberty of Christians is further enlarged, in their freedom from the yoke of a ceremonial law, to which the Jewish church was subjected, and in greater boldness of access to the throne of grace, and in fuller communications of the free Spirit of God, than believers under the law did ordinarily partake of.[101]

2. GOD ALONE IS LORD of the conscience, and hath left it free

from the doctrines and commandments of men which are in any thing contrary to his word, or not contained in it. So that to believe such doctrines, or obey such commands out of conscience, is to betray true liberty of conscience; and the requiring of an implicit faith, an absolute and blind obedience, is to destroy liberty of conscience and reason also.[102]

3. THEY WHO upon pretence of Christian liberty do practice any sin, or cherish any sinful lust, as they do thereby pervert the main design of the grace of the gospel to their own destruction, so they wholly destroy the end of Christian liberty, which is, that being delivered out of the hands of all our enemies, we might serve the Lord without fear, in holiness and righteousness before him, all the days of our lives.[103]

22. Of Religious Worship and the Sabbath Day

1. THE LIGHT OF NATURE shows that there is a God, who hath lordship and sovereignty over all; is just, good and doth good unto all; and is therefore to be feared, loved, praised, called upon, trusted in, and served, with all the heart and all the soul, and with all the might. But the acceptable way of worshipping the true God, is instituted by himself, and so limited by his own revealed will, that he may not be worshipped according to the imagination and devices of men, nor the suggestions of Satan, under any visible representations, or any other way not prescribed in the Holy Scriptures.[104]

2. RELIGIOUS WORSHIP is to be given to God the Father, Son, and Holy Spirit, and to him alone; not to angels, saints, or any other creatures; and since the fall, not without a mediator, nor in the mediation of any other but Christ alone.[105]

3. PRAYER, with thanksgiving, being one part of natural worship, is by God required of all men. But that it may be accepted, it is to be made in the name of the Son, by the help of the Spirit, according to his will; with understanding, reverence, humility, fervency, faith, love, and perseverance; and when with others, in a known tongue.[106]

4. PRAYER is to be made for things lawful, and for all sorts of men living, or that shall live hereafter; but not for the dead, nor for those of whom it may be known that they have sinned the sin unto death.[107]

5. THE READING OF THE SCRIPTURES, preaching, and hearing the Word of God, teaching and admonishing one another in psalms, hymns, and spiritual songs, singing with grace in our hearts to the Lord; as also the administration of baptism, and the Lord's Supper, are all parts of religious worship of God, to be performed in obedience to him, with understanding, faith, reverence, and godly fear; moreover, solemn humiliation, with fastings, and thanksgivings, upon special occasions, ought to be used in an holy and religious manner.[108]

6. NEITHER PRAYER nor any other part of religious worship, is now under the gospel, tied unto, or made more acceptable by any place in which it is performed, or towards which it is directed; but God is to be worshipped everywhere in spirit and in truth; as in private families daily, and in secret each one by himself; so more solemnly in the public assemblies, which are not carelessly nor willfully to be neglected or forsaken, when God by His Word or providence calleth thereunto.[109]

7. AS IT IS THE LAW of nature, that in general a proportion of time, by God's appointment, be set apart for the worship of God, so by his Word, in a positive moral, and perpetual commandment, binding all men, in all ages, he hath particularly appointed one day in seven for a sabbath to be kept holy unto him, which from the beginning of the world to the resurrection of Christ was the last day of the week, and from the resurrection of Christ was changed into the first day of the week, which is called the Lord's day: and is to be continued to the end of the world as the Christian sabbath, the observation of the last day of the week being abolished.[110]

8. THE SABBATH is then kept holy unto the Lord, when men, after a due preparing of their hearts, and ordering their common affairs aforehand, do not only observe an holy rest all day, from their own works, words and thoughts, about their worldly

employment and recreations, but are also taken up the whole time in the public and private exercises of his worship, and in the duties of necessity and mercy.[111]

23. Of Singing of Psalms, &c.

WE BELIEVE THAT SINGING the praises of God,[112] is a holy ordinance of Christ, and not a part of natural religion, or a moral duty only; but that it is brought under divine institution, it being injoined on the churches of Christ to sing psalms, hymns, and spiritual songs; and that the whole church in their publick assemblies (as well as private Christians) ought to sing God's praises according to the best light they have received.[113] Moreover, it was practised in the great representative church, by our Lord Jesus Christ with his disciples,[114] after he had instituted and celebrated the sacred ordinance of his Holy Supper, as a commemorative token of redeeming love.

24. Of Lawful Oaths and Vows

1. A LAWFUL OATH is a part of religious worship, wherein the person swearing in truth, righteousness, and judgment, solemnly calleth God to witness what he sweareth, and to judge him according to the truth or falseness thereof.[115]

2. THE NAME OF GOD only is that by which men ought to swear; and therein it is to be used, with all holy fear and reverence; therefore to swear vainly or rashly by that glorious and dreadful name, or to swear at all by any other thing, is sinful, and to be abhorred; yet as in matter of weight and moment, for confirmation of truth, and ending all strife, an oath is warranted by the word of God; so a lawful oath being imposed by lawful authority in such matters, ought to be taken.[116]

3. WHOSOEVER taketh an oath warranted by the Word of God, ought duly to consider the weightiness of so solemn an act, and therein to avouch nothing but what he knoweth to be truth; for that by rash, false, and vain oaths, the Lord is provoked, and

for them this land mourns.[117]

4. AN OATH is to be taken in the plain and common sense of the words, without equivocation or mental reservation.[118]

5. A VOW, which is not to be made to any creature, but to God alone, is to be made and performed with all religious care and faithfulness; but popish monastical vows of perpetual single life, professed poverty, and regular obedience, are so far from being degrees of higher perfection, that they are superstitious and sinful snares, in which no Christian may entangle himself.[119]

25. Of the Civil Magistrate

1. GOD, THE SUPREME LORD AND KING of all the world, hath ordained civil magistrates to be under him, over the people, for his own glory and the public good; and to this end hath armed them with the power of the sword, for defense and encouragement of them that do good, and for the punishment of evil doers.[120]

2. IT IS LAWFUL for Christians to accept and execute the office of a magistrate when called there unto; in the management whereof, as they ought especially to maintain justice and peace, according to the wholesome laws of each kingdom and commonwealth, so for that end they may lawfully now, under the New Testament wage war upon just and necessary occasions.[121]

3. CIVIL MAGISTRATES being set up by God for the ends aforesaid; subjection, in all lawful things commanded by them, ought to be yielded by us in the Lord, not only for wrath, but for conscience sake; and we ought to make supplications and prayers for kings and all that are in authority, that under them we may live a quiet and peaceable life, in all godliness and honesty.[122]

26. Of Marriage

1. MARRIAGE is to be between one man and one woman; neither is it lawful for any man to have more than one wife, nor for any woman to have more than one husband at the same

time.[123]

2. MARRIAGE was ordained for the mutual help of husband and wife, for the increase of mankind with a legitimate issue, and the preventing of uncleanness.[124]

3. IT IS LAWFUL for all sorts of people to marry, who are able with judgment to give their consent; yet it is the duty of Christians to marry in the Lord; and therefore such as profess the true religion, should not marry with infidels, or idolaters; neither should such as are godly, be unequally yoked, by marrying with such as are wicked in their life, or maintain damnable heresy.[125]

4. MARRIAGE ought not to be within the degrees of consanguinity or affinity, forbidden in the Word; nor can such incestuous marriages ever be made lawful, by any law of man or consent of parties, so as those persons may live together as man and wife.[126]

27. Of the Church

1. THE CATHOLIC OR UNIVERSAL CHURCH, which (with respect to the internal work of the Spirit and truth of grace) may be called invisible, consists of the whole number of the elect, that have been, are, or shall be gathered into one, under Christ, the head thereof; and is the spouse, the body, the fullness of him that filleth all in all.[127]

2. ALL PERSONS throughout the world, professing the faith of the gospel, and obedience unto God by Christ according unto it, not destroying their own profession by any errors averting the foundation, or unholiness of conversation, are and may be called visible saints; and of such ought all particular congregations to be constituted.[128]

3. THE PUREST CHURCHES under heaven are subject to mixture and error; and some have so degenerated as to become no churches of Christ, but synagogues of Satan; nevertheless Christ always hath had, and ever shall have a kingdom in this world, to the end thereof, of such as believe in him, and make profession of his name.[129]

4. THE LORD JESUS CHRIST is the Head of the church, in whom, by the appointment of the Father, all power for the calling, institution, order or government of the church, is invested in a supreme and sovereign manner; neither can the Pope of Rome in any sense be head thereof, but is that antichrist, that man of sin, and son of perdition, that exalteth himself in the church against Christ, and all that is called God; whom the Lord shall destroy with the brightness of his coming.[130]

5. IN THE EXECUTION of this power wherewith he is so entrusted, the Lord Jesus calleth out of the world unto himself, through the ministry of his word, by his Spirit, those that are given unto him by his Father, that they may walk before him in all the ways of obedience, which he prescribeth to them in his Word. Those thus called, he commandeth to walk together in particular societies, or churches, for their mutual edification, and the due performance of that public worship, which he requireth of them in the world.[131]

6. THE MEMBERS of these churches are saints by calling, visibly manifesting and evidencing (in and by their profession and walking) their obedience unto that call of Christ; and do willingly consent to walk together, according to the appointment of Christ; giving up themselves to the Lord, and one to another, by the will of God, in professed subjection to the ordinances of the gospel.[132]

7. TO EACH of these churches thus gathered, according to his mind declared in his Word, he hath given all that power and authority, which is in any way needful for their carrying on that order in worship and discipline, which he hath instituted for them to observe; with commands and rules for the due and right exerting, and executing of that power.[133]

8. A PARTICULAR CHURCH, gathered and completely organized according to the mind of Christ, consists of officers and members; and the officers appointed by Christ to be chosen and set apart by the church (so called and gathered), for the peculiar administration of ordinances, and execution of power or duty, which he entrusts them with, or calls them to, to be continued to the end of the world, are bishops or elders, and deacons.[134]

9. THE WAY appointed by Christ for the calling of any person, fitted and gifted by the Holy Spirit, unto the office of bishop or elder in a church, is, that he be chosen thereunto by the common suffrage of the church itself; and solemnly set apart by fasting and prayer, with imposition of hands of the eldership of the church, if there be any before constituted therein; and of a deacon that he be chosen by the like suffrage, and set apart by prayer, and the like imposition of hands.[135]

10. THE WORK OF PASTORS being constantly to attend the service of Christ, in his churches, in the ministry of the word and prayer, with watching for their souls, as they that must give an account to him; it is incumbent on the churches to whom they minister, not only to give them all due respect, but also to communicate to them of all their good things according to their ability, so as they may have a comfortable supply, without being themselves entangled in secular affairs; and may also be capable of exercising hospitality towards others; and this is required by the law of nature, and by the express order of our Lord Jesus, who hath ordained that they that preach the gospel should live of the gospel.[136]

11. ALTHOUGH it be incumbent on the bishops or pastors of the churches, to be instant in preaching the word, by way of office, yet the work of preaching the word is not so peculiarly confined to them but that others also gifted and fitted by the Holy Spirit for it, and approved and called by the church, may and ought to perform it.[137]

12. AS ALL BELIEVERS are bound to join themselves to particular churches, when and where they have opportunity so to do; so all that are admitted unto the privileges of a church, are also under the censures and government thereof, according to the rule of Christ.[138]

13. NO CHURCH MEMBERS, upon any offence taken by them, having performed their duty required of them towards the person they are offended at, ought to disturb any church-order, or absent themselves from the assemblies of the church, or administration of any ordinances, upon the account of such offence at any of their

fellow members, but to wait upon Christ, in the further proceeding of the church.[139]

14. AS EACH CHURCH, and all the members of it, are bound to pray continually for the good and prosperity of all the churches of Christ, in all places, and upon all occasions to further every one within the bounds of their places and callings, in the exercise of their gifts and graces, so the churches, when planted by the providence of God, so as they may enjoy opportunity and advantage for it, ought to hold communion among themselves, for their peace, increase of love, and mutual edification.[140]

15. IN CASES of difficulties or differences, either in point of doctrine or administration, wherein either the churches in general are concerned, or any one church, in their peace, union, and edification; or any member or members of any church are injured, in or by any proceedings in censures not agreeable to truth and order: it is according to the mind of Christ, that many churches holding communion together, do, by their messengers, meet to consider, and give their advice in or about that matter in difference, to be reported to all the churches concerned; howbeit these messengers assembled, are not entrusted with any church-power properly so called; or with any jurisdiction over the churches themselves, to exercise any censures either over any churches or persons; or to impose their determination on the churches or officers.[141]

28. Of the Communion of Saints

1. ALL SAINTS that are united to Jesus Christ, their head, by his Spirit, and faith, although they are not made thereby one person with him, have fellowship in his graces, sufferings, death, resurrection, and glory; and, being united to one another in love, they have communion in each others gifts and graces, and are obliged to the performance of such duties, public and private, in an orderly way, as do conduce to their mutual good, both in the inward and outward man.[142]

2. SAINTS by profession are bound to maintain an holy

fellowship and communion in the worship of God, and in performing such other spiritual services as tend to their mutual edification; as also in relieving each other in outward things according to their several abilities, and necessities; which communion, according to the rule of the gospel, though especially to be exercised by them, in the relation wherein they stand, whether in families, or churches, yet, as God offereth opportunity, is to be extended to all the household of faith, even all those who in every place call upon the name of the Lord Jesus; nevertheless their communion one with another as saints, doth not take away or infringe the title or propriety which each man hath in his goods and possessions.[143]

29. Of Baptism and the Lord's Supper

1. BAPTISM AND THE LORD'S SUPPER are ordinances of positive and sovereign institution, appointed by the Lord Jesus, the only lawgiver, to be continued in his church to the end of the world.[144]

2. THESE HOLY APPOINTMENTS are to be administered by those only who are qualified and thereunto called, according to the commission of Christ.[145]

30. Of Baptism

1. BAPTISM IS AN ORDINANCE of the New Testament, ordained by Jesus Christ, to be unto the party baptized, a sign of his fellowship with him, in his death and resurrection; of his being engrafted into him; of remission of sins; and of giving up into God, through Jesus Christ, to live and walk in newness of life.[146]

2. THOSE WHO do actually profess repentance towards God, faith in, and obedience to, our Lord Jesus Christ, are the only proper subjects of this ordinance.[147]

3. THE OUTWARD ELEMENT to be used in this ordinance is water, wherein the party is to be baptized, in the name of the Father, and of the Son, and of the Holy Spirit.[148]

4. IMMERSION, or dipping of the person in water, is necessary

to the due administration of this ordinance.[149]

31. Of Laying on of Hands

WE BELIEVE THAT LAYING ON OF HANDS (with prayer), upon baptized believers, as such, is an ordinance of Christ,[150] and ought to be submitted unto by all such persons that are admitted to partake of the Lord's Supper; and that the end of this ordinance is not for the extraordinary gifts of the Spirit, but for a farther reception of the Holy Spirit of promise,[151] or for the addition of the graces of the Spirit, and the influences thereof; to confirm, strengthen, and comfort them in Christ Jesus; it being ratified and established by the extraordinary gifts of the Spirit in the primitive times,[152] to abide in the church, as meeting together on the first day of the week was,[153] that being the day of worship, or Christian Sabbath, under the Gospel; and as preaching the word was,[154] and as baptism was,[155] and prayer was,[156] and singing psalms, &c. was,[157] so this, of laying on of hands was.[158] For as the whole Gospel was confirmed by signs and wonders, and divers miracles and gifts of the Holy Ghost in general,[159] so was every ordinance in like manner confirmed in particular.

32. Of the Lord's Supper

1. THE SUPPER OF THE LORD JESUS was instituted by him the same night wherein he was betrayed, to be observed in his churches, unto the end of the world, for the perpetual remembrance, and showing forth the sacrifice of himself in his death, confirmation of the faith of believers in all the benefits thereof, their spiritual nourishment, and growth in him, their further engagement in, and to all duties which they owe to him; and to be a bond and pledge of their communion with him, and with each other.[160]

2. IN THIS ORDINANCE CHRIST is not offered up to his Father, nor any real sacrifice made at all for remission of sin of the quick or dead, but only a memorial of that one offering up of himself by

himself upon the cross, once for all; and a spiritual oblation of all possible praise unto God for the same. So that the popish sacrifice of the mass, as they call it, is most abominable, injurious to Christ's own sacrifice the alone propitiation for all the sins of the elect.[161]

3. THE LORD JESUS HATH, in this ordinance, appointed his ministers to pray, and bless the elements of bread and wine, and thereby to set them apart from a common to a holy use, and to take and break the bread; to take the cup, and, they communicating also themselves, to give both to the communicants.[162]

4. THE DENIAL of the cup to the people, worshipping the elements, the lifting them up, or carrying them about for adoration, and reserving them for any pretended religious use, are all contrary to the nature of this ordinance, and to the institution of Christ.[163]

5. THE OUTWARD ELEMENTS in this ordinance, duly set apart to the use ordained by Christ, have such relation to him crucified, as that truly, although in terms used figuratively, they are sometimes called by the names of the things they represent, to wit, the body and blood of Christ, albeit, in substance and nature, they still remain truly and only bread and wine, as they were before.[164]

6. THAT DOCTRINE which maintains a change of the substance of bread and wine, into the substance of Christ's body and blood, commonly called transubstantiation, by consecration of a priest, or by any other way, is repugnant not to Scripture alone, but even to common sense and reason, overthroweth the nature of the ordinance, and hath been, and is, the cause of manifold superstitions, yea, of gross idolatries.[165]

7. WORTHY RECEIVERS, outwardly partaking of the visible elements in this ordinance, do then also inwardly by faith, really and indeed, yet not carnally and corporally, but spiritually receive, and feed upon Christ crucified, and all the benefits of his death; the body and blood of Christ being then not corporally or carnally, but spiritually present to the faith of believers in that ordinance, as the elements themselves are to their outward

senses.[166]

8. ALL IGNORANT and ungodly persons, as they are unfit to enjoy communion with Christ, so are they unworthy of the Lord's table, and cannot, without great sin against him, while they remain such, partake of these holy mysteries, or be admitted thereunto; yea, whosoever shall receive unworthily, are guilty of the body and blood of the Lord, eating and drinking judgment to themselves.[167]

33. Of Man's State After Death and the Resurrection

1. THE BODIES OF MEN after death return to dust, and see corruption; but their souls, which neither die nor sleep, having an immortal subsistence, immediately return to God who gave them. The souls of the righteous being then made perfect in holiness, are received into paradise, where they are with Christ, and behold the face of God in light and glory, waiting for the full redemption of their bodies; and the souls of the wicked are cast into hell; where they remain in torment and utter darkness, reserved to the judgment of the great day; besides these two places, for souls separated from their bodies, the scripture acknowledgeth none.[168]

2. AT THE LAST DAY, such of the saints as are found alive, shall not sleep, but be changed; and all the dead shall be raised up with the selfsame bodies, and none other; although with different qualities, which shall be united again to their souls forever.[169]

3. THE BODIES of the unjust shall, by the power of Christ, be raised to dishonor; the bodies of the just, by his Spirit, unto honor, and be made conformable to his own glorious body.[170]

34. Of the Last Judgment

1. GOD HATH APPOINTED A DAY wherein he will judge the world in righteousness, by Jesus Christ; to whom all power and judgment is given of the Father; in which day, not only the apostate angels shall be judged, but likewise all persons that have lived upon the earth shall appear before the tribunal of Christ, to

give an account of their thoughts, words, and deeds, and to receive according to what they have done in the body, whether good or evil.[171]

2. THE END of God's appointing this day, is for the manifestation of the glory of his mercy, in the eternal salvation of the elect; and of his justice, in the eternal damnation of the reprobate, who are wicked and disobedient; for then shall the righteous go into everlasting life, and receive that fullness of joy and glory with everlasting rewards, in the presence of the Lord; but the wicked, who know not God, and obey not the gospel of Jesus Christ, shall be cast aside into everlasting torments, and punished with everlasting destruction, from the presence of the Lord, and from the glory of his power.[172]

3. AS CHRIST would have us to be certainly persuaded that there shall be a day of judgment, both to deter all men from sin, and for the greater consolation of the godly in their adversity, so will he have the day unknown to men, that they may shake off all carnal security, and be always watchful, because they know not at what hour the Lord will come, and may ever be prepared to say, Come Lord Jesus; come quickly. Amen.[173]

---

1 2 Timothy 3:15-17; Isaiah 8:20; Luke 16:29, 31; Ephesians 2:20; Romans 1:19-21; 2:14-15; Psalm 19:1-3; Proverbs 22:19-21; Romans 15:4; Hebrews 1:1; 2 Peter 1:19-20

2 2 Timothy 3:16

3 Luke 24:27, 44; Romans 3:2

4 2 Thessalonians 2:13; 2 Timothy 3:16; 2 Peter 1:19-21; 1 John 5:9

5 John 16:13, 14; 1 Corinthians 2:10-12; 1 John 2:20, 27

6 2 Timothy 3:15-17; Galatians 1:8, 9; John 6:45; 1 Corinthians 2:9-12; 11:13, 14; 14:26, 40

7 2 Peter 3:16; Psalm 19:7; 119:130;

8 Romans 3:2; Isaiah 8:20; Acts 15:15; John 5:39; 1 Corinthians 14:6, 9, 11, 12, 24, 28; Colossians 3:16

9 2 Peter 1:20, 21; Acts 15:15, 16

10 Matthew 22:29, 31, 32; Ephesians 2:20; Acts 28:23

11 1 Corinthians 8:4, 8; Deuteronomy 6:4; Jeremiah 10:10; Isaiah 48:12; Exodus 3:14; John 4:24; 1 Timothy 1:17; Deuteronomy 4:15, 16; Malachi 3:6; 1 Kings 8:27; Jeremiah 23:23; Psalms 90:2; Genesis 17:1; Isaiah 6:3; Psalms 115:3; Isaiah 46:10; Proverbs 16:4; Romans 11:36; Exodus 34:6, 7; Hebrews 11:6; Nehemiah 9:32, 33; Psalm 5:5, 6; Exodus 34:7; Nahum 1:2, 3

12 John 5:26; Psalms 148:13; Psalms 119:68; Job 22:2, 3; Romans 11:34-36; Daniel 4:25, 34, 35; Hebrews 4:13; Ezekiel 11:5; Acts 15:18; Psalms 145:17; Revelation 5:12-14

13 1 John 5:7; Matthew 28:19; 2 Corinthians 13:14; Exodus 3:14; John 14:11; 1 Corinthians 8:6; John 1:14, 18; John 15:26; Galatians 4:6

14 Isaiah 46:10; Ephesians 1:11; Hebrews 6:17; Romans 9:15, 18; James 1:13; 1 John 1:5; Acts 4:27, 28; John 19:11; Numbers 23:19; Ephesians 1:3-5

15 Acts 15:18; Romans 9:11, 13, 16, 18

16 1 Timothy 5:21; Matthew 25:34; Ephesians 1:5, 6; Romans 9:22, 23; Jude 4

17 2 Timothy 2:19; John 13:18;

18 Ephesians 1:4, 9, 11; Romans 8:30; 2 Timothy 1:9; 1 Thessalonians 5:9; Romans 9:13, 16; Ephesians 2:5, 12

19 1 Peter 1:2; 2 Thessalonians 2:13; 1 Thessalonians 5:9; Romans 8:30; 2 Thessalonians 2:13; 1 Peter 1: 5; John 10:26; John 17:9; John 6:64

20 1 Thessalonians 1:4, 5; 2 Peter 1:10; Ephesians 1:6; Romans 11:33; Romans 11:5, 6, 20; Luke 10:20

21 John 1:2, 3; Hebrews 1:2; Job 26:13; Romans 1:20; Colossians 1:16; Genesis 1:31

22 Genesis 1:27; Genesis 2:7; Ecclesiastes 7:29; Genesis 1:26; Romans 2:14, 15; Genesis 3:6

23 Genesis 2:17; Genesis 1:26, 28

24 Hebrews 1:3; Job 38:11; Isaiah 46:10; Psalm 135:6; Matthew 10:29-31; Ephesians 1:11

25 Acts 2:23; Proverbs 16:33; Genesis 8:22

26 Acts 27:31, 44; Isaiah 55:10; Hosea 1:7; Romans 4:9-21; Daniel 3:27

27 Romans 11:32-34; 2 Samuel 24:1; 1 Chronicles 21:1; 2 Kings 19:28; Psalms 76:10; Genesis 1:20; Isaiah 10:6, 7, 12; Psalms 1:21; 1 John 2:16

28 2 Chronicles 32:25, 26, 31; 2 Corinthians 12:7-9; Romans 8:28

29 Romans 1:24-26, 28; Romans 11:7, 8; Deuteronomy 29:4; Matthew 13:12; Deuteronomy 2:30; 2 Kings 8:12, 13; Psalms 81:11, 12; 2 Thessalonians 2:10-12; Exodus 8:15, 32; Isaiah 6:9, 10; 1 Peter 2:7, 8

[30] 1 Timothy 4:10; Amos 9:8, 9; Isaiah 43:3-5

[31] Genesis 2:16, 17; Genesis 3:12, 13; 2 Corinthians 11:3

[32] Romans 3:23; Romans 5:12 &etc; Titus 1:15; Genesis 6:5; Jeremiah 17:9; Romans 3:10-19

[33] Romans 5:12-19; 1 Corinthians 15:21, 22, 45, 49; Psalms 51:5; Job 14:4; Ephesians 2:3; Romans 6:20; Romans 5:12; Hebrews 2:14, 15; 1 Thessalonians 1:10

[34] Romans 8:7; Colossians 1:21; James 1:14, 15; Matthew 15:19

[35] Romans 7:18, 23; Ecclesiastes 7:20; 1 John 1:8; Romans 7:23-25; Galatians 5:17

[36] Luke 17:10; Job 35:7, 8

[37] Genesis 2:17; Galatians 3:10; Romans 3:20, 21; Romans 8:3; Mark 16:15, 16; John 3:16; Ezekiel 36:26; John 6:44; Psalm 110:3

[38] Genesis 3:15; Hebrews 1:1; 2 Timothy 1:9; Titus 1:2; Hebrews 11:6, 13; Romans 4:1, 2 &etc; Acts 4:12; John 8:56

[39] Isaiah 42:1; 1 Peter 1:19, 20; Acts 3:22; Hebrews 5:5, 6; Psalm 2:6; Luke 1:33; Ephesians 1:22, 23; Hebrews 1:2; Acts 17:31; Isaiah 53:10; John 17:6; Romans 8:30

[40] John 1:14; Galatians 4:4; Romans 8:3; Hebrews 2:14, 16, 17; Hebrews 4:15; Matthew 1:22, 23; Luke 1:27, 31, 35; Romans 9:5; 1 Timothy 2:5

[41] Psalms 45:7; Acts 10:38; John 3:34; Colossians 1:9; 2:3; Hebrews 7:26; John 1:14; Hebrews 5:5; 7:22; John 5:22, 27; Matthew 28:18; Acts 2:36

[42] Psalm 40:7, 8; Hebrews 10:5-10; John 10:18; Galatians 4:4; Matthew 3:15; Galatians 3:13; Isaiah 53:6; 1 Peter 3:18; 2 Corinthians 5:21; Matthew 26:37, 38; Luke 22:44; Matthew 27:46; Acts 13:37; 1 Corinthians 15:3, 4; John 20:25, 27; Mark 16:19; Acts 1:9-11; Romans 8:34; Hebrews 9:24; Acts 10:42; Romans 14:9, 10; Acts 1:11; 2 Peter 2:4

[43] Hebrews 9:14; 10:14; Romans 3:25, 26; John 17:2; Hebrews 9:15

[44] 1 Corinthians 4:10; Hebrews 4:2; 1 Peter 1:10, 11; Revelation 13:8; Hebrews 13:8

[45] John 3:13; Acts 20:28

[46] John 6:37; 10:15, 16; 17:9; Romans 5:10; John 17:6; Ephesians 1:9; 1 John 5:20; Romans 8:9, 14; Psalm 110:1; 1 Corinthians 15:25, 26; John 3:8; Ephesians 1:8

[47] 1 Timothy 2:5

[48] John 1:18; Colossians 1:21; Galatians 5:17; Psalms 110:3; John 16:8; Luke 1:74, 75

[49] Matthew 17:12; James 1:14; Deuteronomy 30:19

[50] Ecclesiastes 7:29; Genesis 3:6

[51] John 6:44; Romans 5:6; 8:7; Ephesians 2:1, 5; Titus 3:3-5

52 Colossians 1:13; John 8:36; Philippians 2:13; Romans 7:15, 18, 19, 21, 23

53 Ephesians 4:13

54 Romans 8:30; 11:7; Ephesians 1:10, 11; 2 Thessalonians 2:13, 14; Ephesians 2:1-6; Acts 26:18; Ephesians 1:17; Ezekiel 36:26; Deuteronomy 30:6; Ezekiel 36:27; Ephesians 1:19; Psalm 110:3; Song of Songs 1:4

55 2 Timothy 1:9; Ephesians 2:8; 1 Corinthians 2:14; Ephesians 2:5; John 5:25; Ephesians 1:19, 20

56 John 3:3, 5, 6, 8

57 Matthew 22:14; Matthew 13:20, 21; Hebrews 6:4, 5; John 6:44, 45, 65; 1 John 2:24, 25; Acts 4:12; John 4:22; John 17:3

58 Romans 3:24; Romans 8:30; Romans 4:5-8; Ephesians 1:7; 1 Corinthians 1:30, 31; Romans 5:17-19; Philippians 3:8, 9; Ephesians 2:8-10; John 1:12; Romans 5:17

59 Romans 3:28; Galatians 5:6; James 2:17, 22, 26

60 Hebrews 10:14; 1 Peter 1:18, 19; Isaiah 53:5, 6; Romans 8:32; 2 Corinthians 5:21; Romans 3:26; Ephesians 1:6, 7; Ephesians 2:7

61 Galatians 3:8; 1 Peter 1:2; 1 Timothy 2:6; Romans 4:25; Colossians 1:21, 22; Titus 3:4-7

62 Matthew 6:12; 1 John 1:7, 9; John 10:28; Psalm 89:31-33; Psalm 32:5; Psalm 51: 1-19; Matthew 26:75

63 Galatians 3:9; Romans 4:22-24

64 Ephesians 1:5; Galatians 4:4, 5; John 1:12; Romans 8:17; 2 Corinthians 6:18; Revelation 3:12; Romans 8:15; Galatians 4:6; Ephesians 2:18; Psalm 103:13; Proverbs 14:26; 1 Peter 5:7; Hebrews 12:6; Isaiah 54:8, 9; Lamentations 3:31; Ephesians 4:30; Hebrews 1:14; Hebrews 6:12

65 Acts 20:32; Romans 6:5, 6; John 17:17; Ephesians 3:16-19; 1 Thessalonians 5:21-23; Romans 6:14; Galatians 5:24; Colossians 1:11; 2 Corinthians 7:1; Hebrews 12:14

66 1 Thessalonians 5:23; Romans 7:18, 23; Galatians 5:17; 1 Peter 2:11

67 Romans 7:23; Romans 6:14; Ephesians 4:15, 16; 2 Corinthians 3:18; 2 Corinthians 7:1

68 2 Corinthians 4:13; Ephesians 2:8; Romans 10:14, 17; Luke 17:5; 1 Peter 2:2; Acts 20:32

69 Acts 24:14; Psalm 27:7-10; Psalm 119:72; 2 Timothy 1:12; John 14:14; Isaiah 66:2; Hebrews 11:13; John 1:12; Acts 16:31; Galatians 2:20; Acts 15:11

70 Hebrews 5:13, 14; Matthew 6:30; Romans 4:19, 20; 2 Peter 1:1; Ephesians 6:16; 1 John 5:4, 5; Hebrews 6:11, 12; Colossians 2:2; Hebrews 12:2

[71] Titus 3:2-5

[72] Ecclesiastes 7:20; Luke 22:31, 32

[73] Zechariah 12:10; Acts 11:18; Ezekiel 36:31; 2 Corinthians 7:11; Psalm 119:6, 128

[74] Luke 19:8; 1 Timothy 1:13, 15

[75] Romans 6:23; Isaiah 1:16-18; Isaiah 55:7

[76] Micah 6:8; Hebrews 13:21; Matthew 15:9; Isaiah 29:13

[77] James 2:18, 22; Psalm 116:12, 13; 1 John 2:3, 5; 2 Peter 1:5-11; Matthew 5:16; 1 Timothy 6:1; 1 Peter 2:15; Philippians 1:11; Ephesians 2:10; Romans 6:22

[78] John 15:4, 5; 2 Corinthians 3:5; Philippians 2:13; Philippians 2:12; Hebrews 6:11, 12; Isaiah 64:7

[79] Job 9:2, 3; Galatians 5:17; Luke 17:10

[80] Romans 3:20; Ephesians 2:8, 9; Romans 4:6; Galatians 5:22, 23; Isaiah 64:6; Psalms 143:2

[81] Ephesians 1:6; 1 Peter 2:5; Matthew 25:21, 23; Hebrews 6:10

[82] 2 Kings 10:31; 1 Kings 21:27, 29; Genesis 4:5; Hebrews 11:4, 6; 1 Corinthians 13:1; Matthew 6:2, 5; Amos 5:21, 22; Romans 9:16; Titus 3:5; Job 21:14, 15; Matthew 25:41-43

[83] John 10:28; Philippians 1:6; 2 Timothy 2:19; 1 John 2:19; Psalm 89:31, 32; 1 Corinthians 11:32; Malachi 3:6

[84] Romans 8:30; Romans 9:11, 16; Romans 5:9, 10; John 14:19; Hebrews 6:17, 18; 1 John 3:9; Jeremiah 32:40

[85] Matthew 26:70, 72, 74; Isaiah 64:5, 9; Ephesians 4:30; Psalm 51:10; Psalm 32:3, 4; 2 Samuel 12:14; Luke 22:32, 61, 62

[86] Job 8:13, 14; Matthew 7:22, 23; 1 John 2:3; 1 John 3:14, 18, 19, 21, 24; 1 John 5:13; Romans 5:2, 5

[87] Hebrews 6:11, 19; Hebrews 6:17, 18; 2 Peter 1:4, 5, 10, 11; Romans 8:15, 16; 1 John 3:1-3

[88] Isaiah 50:10; Psalm 88:1-18; Psalm 77:1-12; 1 John 4:13; Hebrews 6:11, 12; Romans 5:1, 2, 5; Romans 14:17; Psalm 119:32; Romans 6:1, 2; Titus 2:11, 12, 14

[89] Song of Songs 5:2, 3, 6; Psalm 51:8, 12, 14; Psalm 116:11; Psalm 77:7, 8; Psalm 31:22; Psalm 30:7; 1 John 3:9; Luke 22:32; Psalm 42:5, 11; Lamentation 3:26-31

[90] Genesis 1:27; Ecclesiastes 7:29; Romans 10:5; Galatians 3:10, 12

[91] Romans 2:14, 15; Deuteronomy 10:4

[92] Hebrews 10:1; Colossians 2:17; 1 Corinthians 5:7; Colossians 2:14, 16, 17; Ephesians

2:14, 16

93 1 Corinthians 9:8-10

94 Matthew 5:17-19; Romans 3:31; 13:8-10; James 2:8, 10-12

95 Romans 6:12-14; Galatians 2:16; Romans 8:1; Romans 10:4; Romans 3:20; Romans 7:7, &etc.; 1 Peter 3:8-13

96 Galatians 3:21; Ezekiel 36:37

97 Genesis 3:15; Revelation 13:8

98 Romans 1:17; Romans 10:14, 15, 17; Proverbs 29:18; Isaiah 25:7; Isaiah 60:2, 3

99 Psalm 147:20; Acts 16:7; Romans 1:18-32

100 Psalm 110:3; 1 Corinthians 2:14; Ephesians 1:19, 20; John 6:44; 2 Corinthians 4:4, 6

101 Galatians 3:13; Galatians 1:4; Acts 26:18; Romans 8:3; Romans 8:28; 1 Corinthians 15:54-57; 2 Thessalonians 1:10; Romans 8:15; Luke 1:73-75; 1 John 4:8; Galatians 3:9, 14; John 7:38, 39; Hebrews 10:19-21

102 James 4:12; Romans 14:4; Acts 4:19, 29; 1 Corinthians 7:23; Matthew 15:9; Colossians 2:20, 22, 23; 1 Corinthians 3:5; 2 Corinthians 1:24

103 Romans 6:1, 2; Galatians 5:13; 2 Peter 2:18, 21

104 Jeremiah 10:7; Mark 12:33; Deuteronomy 12:32; Exodus 20:4-6

105 Matthew 4:9, 10; John 6:23; Matthew 28:19; Romans 1:25; Colossians 2:18; Revelation 19:10; John 14:6; 1 Timothy 2:5

106 Psalm 95:1-7; Psalm 65:2; John 14:13, 14; 1 John 5:14; Romans 8:26; 1 Corinthians 14:16, 17

107 1 Timothy 2:1, 2; 2 Samuel 7:29; 2 Samuel 12:21-23; 1 John 5:16

108 1 Timothy 4:13; 2 Timothy 4:2; Luke 8:18; Colossians 3:16; Ephesians 5:19; Matthew 28:19, 20; 1 Corinthians 11:26; Esther 4:16; Joel 2:12; Exodus 15:1-19; Psalm 107:1-43

109 John 4:21; Malachi 1:11; 1 Timothy 2:8; Acts 10:2; Matthew 6:11; Psalm 55:17; Matthew 6:6; Hebrews 10:25; Acts 2:42

110 Exodus 20:8; 1 Corinthians 16:1, 2; Acts 20:7; Revelation 1:10

111 Isaiah 58:13; Nehemiah 13:15-22; Matthew 12:1-13

112 Acts 16:25; Ephesians 5:19; Colossians 3:16

113 Hebrews 2:12; James 5:13

114 Matthew 26:30

115 Exodus 20:7; Deuteronomy 10:20; Jeremiah 4:2; 2 Chronicles 6:22, 33

[116] Matthew 5:34, 37; James 5:12; Hebrews 6:16; 2 Corinthians 1:23; Nehemiah 13:25

[117] Leviticus 19:12; Jeremiah 23:10

[118] Psalm 24:4

[119] Psalm 76:11; Genesis 28:20-22; 1 Corinthians 7:2, 9; Ephesians 4:28; Matthew 19:11

[120] Romans 13:1-4

[121] Psalm 82:3; 2 Samuel 23:3; Luke 3:14

[122] Romans 13:5-7; 1 Peter 2:17; 1 Timothy 2:1, 2

[123] Genesis 2:24; Malachi 2:15; Matthew 19:5, 6

[124] Genesis 2:18; Genesis 1:28; 1 Corinthians 7:2, 9

[125] Hebrews 13:4; 1 Timothy 4:3; 1 Corinthians 7:39; Nehemiah 13:15-27

[126] Leviticus 18:1-30; Mark 6:18; 1 Corinthians 5:1

[127] Hebrews 12:23; Colossians 1:18; Ephesians 1:10, 22, 23; Ephesians 5:23, 27, 32

[128] 1 Corinthians 1:2; Acts 11:26; Romans 1:7; Ephesians 1:20-22

[129] 1 Corinthians 5; Revelation 2; Revelation 3; Revelation 18:2; 2 Thessalonians 2:11, 12; Matthew 16:18; Psalm 72:17; Psalm 102:28; Revelation 12:17

[130] Matthew 28:18-20; Ephesians 4:11, 12; Colossians 1:18; 2 Thessalonians 2:2-9

[131] John 10:16; John 12:32; Matthew 28:20; Matthew 18:15-20

[132] Romans 1:7; 1 Corinthians 1:2; Acts 2:41, 42; Acts 5:13, 14; 2 Corinthians 9:13

[133] Matthew 18:17, 18; 1 Corinthians 5:4, 5; 1 Corinthians 5:13; 2 Corinthians 2:6-8

[134] Acts 20:17, 28; Philippians 1:1

[135] Acts 14:23; 1 Timothy 4:14; Acts 6:3, 5, 6

[136] Acts 6:4; Hebrews 13:17; 1 Timothy 5:17, 18; Galatians 6:6, 7; 2 Timothy 2:4; 1 Timothy 3:2; 1 Corinthians 9:6-14

[137] Acts 11:19-21; 1 Peter 4:10, 11

[138] 1 Thessalonians 5:14; 2 Thessalonians 3:6, 14, 15

[139] Matthew 18:15-17; Ephesians 4:2, 3

[140] Ephesians 6:18; Psalm 122:6; Romans 16:1, 2; 3 John 8-10

[141] Acts 15:2, 4, 6, 22, 23, 25; 2 Corinthians 1:24; 1 John 4:1

[142] 1 John 1:3; John 1:16; Philippians 3:10; Romans 6:5, 6; Ephesians 4:15, 16; 1 Corinthians 12:7; 1 Corinthians 3:21-23; 1 Thessalonians 5:11; Romans 1:12; 1 John 3:17,

18; Galatians 6:10

143 Hebrews 10:24, 25; Hebrews 3:12, 13; Acts 11:29, 30; Ephesians 6:4; 1 Corinthians 12:14-27; Acts 5:4; Ephesians 4:28

144 Matthew 28:19, 20; 1 Corinthians 11:26

145 Matthew 28:19; 1 Corinthians 4:1

146 Romans 6:3-5; Colossians 2:12; Galatians 3:27; Mark 1:4; Acts 22:16; Romans 6:4

147 Mark 16:16; Acts 8:36; Acts 2:41; Acts 8:12; Acts 18:18

148 Matthew 28:19, 20; Acts 8:38

149 Matthew 3:16; John 3:23

150 Acts 8:17, 18; Acts 19:6; Hebrews 5:12; Hebrews 6:1, 2

151 Ephesians 1:13,14

152 Acts 18:7, 19:6

153 Acts 2:1

154 Acts 10:44

155 Matthew 3:16

156 Acts 4:31

157 Acts 16:25, 26

158 Acts 8 & 19

159 Hebrews 2:3, 4

160 1 Corinthians 11:23-26; 1 Corinthians 10:16, 17, 21

161 Hebrews 9:25, 26, 28; 1 Corinthians 11:24; Matthew 26:26, 27

162 1 Corinthians 11:23-26

163 Matthew 26:26-28; Matthew 15:9; Exodus 20:4, 5

164 1 Corinthians 11:27; 1 Corinthians 11:26-28

165 Acts 3:21; Luke 14:6; 1 Corinthians 11:24, 25

166 1 Corinthians 10:16; 1 Corinthians 11:23-26

167 2 Corinthians 6:14, 15; 1 Corinthians 11:29; Matthew 7:6

168 Genesis 3:19; Ecclesiastes 12:7; Luke 16:23, 24; 23:43; Acts 13:36; 2 Corinthians 5:1, 6, 8; Philippians 1:23; Hebrews 12:23; 1 Peter 3:19; Jude 6, 7

[169] 1 Corinthians 15:51, 52; 1 Thessalonians 4:17; Job 19:26, 27; 1 Corinthians 15:42, 43

[170] Acts 24:15; John 5:28, 29; Philippians 3:21

[171] Acts 17:31; John 5:22, 27; 1 Corinthians 6:3; Jude 6; 2 Corinthians 5:10; Ecclesiastes 12:14; Matthew 12:36; Romans 14:10, 12; Matthew 25:32-46

[172] Romans 9:22, 23; Matthew 25:21, 34; 2 Timothy 4:8; Matthew 25:46; Mark 9:48; 2 Thessalonians 1:7-10

[173] 2 Corinthians 5:10, 11; 2 Thessalonians 1:5-7; Mark 13:35-37; Luke 12:35-40; Revelation 22:20

Selected Hymns and Psalms

The hymns selected for this devotional booklet are classic, well-known hymns with great theological truth. Among the hymn writers included in this volume are Martin Luther, John Bunyan, John Newton, William Cowper, and Augustus Toplady.

The Scottish Psalter was written anonymously in 1635 and published and appointed for use in worship by the Church of Scotland in 1650. Scripture paraphrases were added in 1781. The Scottish Psalter and Paraphrases was the primary hymnal used by the Church of Scotland through the 19th century. The Scottish Psalter was originally contained in one volume. When the Scripture paraphrases were added in the 18th century, its addition expanded the singular volume.

SELECTIONS

"Faith's Review and Expectation"

also known as "Amazing Grace"
by John Newton (1725-1807)
C.M. 8.6.8.6. (New Britain)

Amazing grace! How sweet the sound,
That saved a wretch like me!
I once was lost but now am found
Was blind, but now I see.

'Twas grace that taught my heart to fear,
And grace my fears relieved;
How precious did that grace appear
The hour I first believed!

Through many dangers, toils, and snares,
I have already come;
'Tis grace hath brought me safe thus far,
And grace will lead me home.

The Lord has promised good to me,
His word my hope secures;
He will my shield and portion be
As long as life endures.

Yes, when this flesh and heart shall fail,
And mortal life shall cease,
I shall possess, within the veil,
A life of joy and peace.

The earth shall soon dissolve like snow,
The sun forbear to shine;
But God, who called me here below,
Will be forever mine.

"A Living and Dying Prayer for the Holiest Believer in the World"

also known as "Rock of Ages"
by Augustus Toplady (1740-1778)
7.7.7.7.7.7. (Toplady)

Rock of Ages, cleft for me,
Let me hide myself in Thee;
Let the water and the blood,
From Thy riven side which flowed,
Be of sin the double cure, Save from wrath and make me pure.

Not the labours of my hands
Can fulfill Thy law's demands;
Could my zeal no respite know,
Could my tears forever flow,
All for sin could not atone: Thou must save, and Thou alone.

Nothing in my hand I bring,
Simply to Thy cross I cling;
Naked, come to Thee for dress;
Helpless, look to Thee for grace;
Foul, I to the fountain fly; Wash me, Saviour, or I die.

While I draw this fleeting breath,
When my eye-strings break in death,
When I soar to worlds unknown,
See Thee on Thy judgment throne;
Rock of Ages, cleft for me, Let me hide myself in Thee.

Then above the world and sin,
Thro' the veil, drawn right within,
I shall see Him face to face,
Sing the story, saved by grace,
Rock of Ages, cleft for me, Let me ever be with Thee.

"Praise for the Fountain Opened"

also known as "There Is a Fountain"
by William Cowper (1731-1800)
C.M.D. 8.6.8.6.D. (Cleansing Fountain)

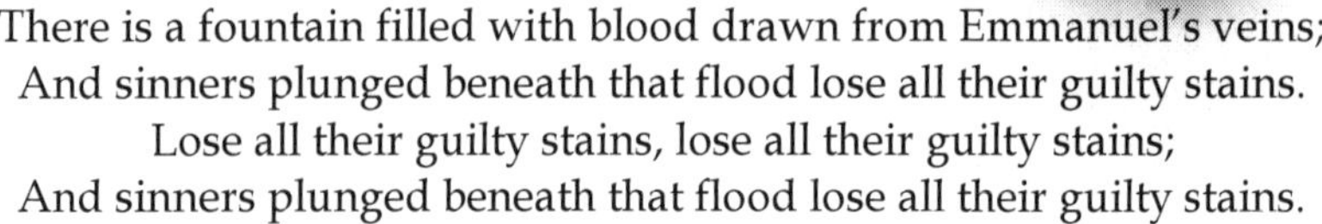

There is a fountain filled with blood drawn from Emmanuel's veins;
And sinners plunged beneath that flood lose all their guilty stains.
Lose all their guilty stains, lose all their guilty stains;
And sinners plunged beneath that flood lose all their guilty stains.

The dying thief rejoiced to see that fountain in his day;
And there have I, though vile as he, washed all my sins away.
Washed all my sins away, washed all my sins away;
And there have I, though vile as he, washed all my sins away.

Dear dying Lamb, Thy precious blood shall never lose its power
Till all the ransomed church of God be saved, to sin no more.
Be saved, to sin no more, be saved, to sin no more;
Till all the ransomed church of God be saved, to sin no more.

E'er since, by faith, I saw the stream Thy flowing wounds supply,
Redeeming love has been my theme, and shall be till I die.
And shall be till I die, and shall be till I die;
Redeeming love has been my theme, and shall be till I die.

Then in a nobler, sweeter song, I'll sing Thy power to save,
When this poor lisping, stammering tongue lies silent in the grave.
Lies silent in the grave, lies silent in the grave;
When this poor lisping, stammering tongue lies silent in the grave.

Lord, I believe Thou hast prepared, unworthy though I be,
For me a blood bought free reward, a golden harp for me!
'Tis strung and tuned for endless years, and formed by power divine,
To sound in God the Father's ears no other name but Thine.

"Exceedingly Great and Precious Promises"

also known as "How Firm a Foundation"
from John Rippon's *Selection of Hymns* (1787) *11.11.11.11.* (Foundation)

How firm a foundation, ye saints of the Lord,
Is laid for your faith in His excellent Word!
What more can He say than to you He hath said,
You, who unto Jesus for refuge have fled?

In every condition, in sickness, in health;
In poverty's vale, or abounding in wealth;
At home and abroad, on the land, on the sea,
As thy days may demand, shall thy strength ever be.

Fear not, I am with thee, O be not dismayed,
For I am thy God and will still give thee aid;
I'll strengthen and help thee, and cause thee to stand
Upheld by My righteous, omnipotent hand.

When through the deep waters I call thee to go,
The rivers of woe shall not thee overflow;
For I will be with thee, thy troubles to bless,
And sanctify to thee thy deepest distress.

When through fiery trials thy pathways shall lie,
My grace, all sufficient, shall be thy supply;
The flame shall not hurt thee; I only design
Thy dross to consume, and thy gold to refine.

Even down to old age all My people shall prove
My sovereign, eternal, unchangeable love;
And when hoary hairs shall their temples adorn,
Like lambs they shall still in My bosom be borne.

The soul that on Jesus has leaned for repose,
I will not, I will not desert to its foes;
That soul, though all hell should endeavor to shake,
I'll never, no never, no never forsake.

"Bí Thusa 'mo Shúile"

traditional Irish hymn also known as "Be Thou My Vision"
translated by Mary Byrne (1880-1931)
10.10.10.10. (Slane)

Be Thou my Vision, O Lord of my heart;
Naught be all else to me, save that Thou art.
Thou my best Thought, by day or by night,
Waking or sleeping, Thy presence my light.

Be Thou my Wisdom, and Thou my true Word;
I ever with Thee and Thou with me, Lord;
Thou my great Father, I Thy true son;
Thou in me dwelling, and I with Thee one.

Be Thou my battle Shield, Sword for the fight;
Be Thou my Dignity, Thou my Delight;
Thou my soul's Shelter, Thou my high Tower:
Raise Thou me heavenward, O Power of my power.

Riches I heed not, nor man's empty praise,
Thou mine Inheritance, now and always:
Thou and Thou only, first in my heart,
High King of Heaven, my Treasure Thou art.

High King of Heaven, my victory won,
May I reach Heaven's joys, O bright Heaven's Sun!
Heart of my own heart, whatever befall,
Still be my Vision, O Ruler of all.

"Who Would True Valour See"

from John Bunyan's book *The Pilgrim's Progress*
by John Bunyan (1628-1688)
6.5.6.5.6.6.6.5. (Monk)

Who would true valour see,
Let him come hither;
One here will constant be,
Come wind, come weather
There's no discouragement
Shall make him once relent
His first avowed intent
To be a pilgrim.

Whoso beset him round
With dismal stories
Do but themselves confound;
His strength the more is.
No lion can him fright,
He'll with a giant fight,
He will have a right
To be a pilgrim.

Hobgoblin nor foul fiend
Can daunt his spirit,
He knows he at the end
Shall life inherit.
Then fancies fly away,
He'll fear not what men say,
He'll labor night and day
To be a pilgrim.

"Ein Feste Burg Ist Unser Gott"

also known as "A Mighty Fortress Is Our God"
by Martin Luther (1483-1546)
translated by Fredrick Hedge (1805-1890)
8.7.8.7.6.6.6.6.7. (Ein Feste Burg)

A mighty fortress is our God, A bulwark never failing;
Our helper He, amid the flood, Of mortal ills prevailing.
For still our ancient foe Doth seek to work us woe;
His craft and pow'r are great,
And, armed with cruel hate,
On earth is not his equal.

Did we in our own strength confide, Our striving would be losing;
Were not the right Man on our side, The Man of God's own choosing.
Dost ask who that may be? Christ Jesus, it is He;
Lord Sabaoth, His name,
From age to age the same,
And He must win the battle.

And tho' this world, with devils filled, Should threaten to undo us,
We will not fear, for God hath willed His truth to triumph thro' us.
The Prince of Darkness grim— We tremble not for him;
His rage we can endure,
For lo, his doom is sure,
One little word shall fell him.

That word above all earthly pow'rs, No thanks to them, abideth;
The Spirit and the gifts are ours Thro' Him who with us sideth.
Let goods and kindred go, This mortal life also;
The body they may kill:
God's truth abideth still,
His kingdom is forever.

Psalms 1

C.M. 8.6.8.6.

1 That man hath perfect blessedness,
who walketh not astray
In counsel of ungodly men,
nor stands in sinners' way,

Nor sitteth in the scorner's chair:
2 But placeth his delight
Upon God's law, and meditates
on his law day and night.

3 He shall be like a tree that grows
near planted by a river,
Which in his season yields his fruit,
and his leaf fadeth never:

And all he doth shall prosper well.
4 The wicked are not so;
But like they are unto the chaff,
which wind drives to and fro.

5 In judgment therefore shall not stand
such as ungodly are;
Nor in th' assembly of the just
shall wicked men appear.

6 For why? the way of godly men
unto the Lord is known:
Whereas the way of wicked men
shall quite be overthrown.

Psalms 6

To the chief Musician on Neginoth upon Sheminith, A Psalm of David.
L.M. 8.8.8.8.

1 Lord, in thy wrath rebuke me not;
Nor in thy hot rage chasten me.
2 Lord, pity me, for I am weak:
Heal me, for my bones vexed be.

3 My soul is also vexed sore;
But, Lord, how long stay wilt thou make?
4 Return, O Lord, my soul set free;
O save me, for thy mercies' sake.

5 Because those that deceased are
Of thee shall no remembrance have;
And who is he that will to thee
Give praises lying in the grave?

6 I with my groaning weary am,
I also all the night my bed
Have caused for to swim; and I
With tears my couch have watered.

7 Mine eye, consum'd with grief, grows old,
Because of all mine enemies.
8 Hence from me, wicked workers all;
For God hath heard my weeping cries.

9 God hath my supplication heard,
My pray'r received graciously
10 Sham'd and sore vex'd be all my foes,
Sham'd and back turned suddenly.

Psalms 23

A Psalm of David.
C.M. 8.6.8.6.

1 The Lord's my shepherd, I'll not want.
2 He makes me down to lie
In pastures green: he leadeth me
the quiet waters by.

3 My soul he doth restore again;
and me to walk doth make
Within the paths of righteousness,
ev'n for his own name's sake.

4 Yea, though I walk in death's dark vale,
yet will I fear none ill:
For thou art with me; and thy rod
and staff me comfort still.

5 My table thou hast furnished
in presence of my foes;
My head thou dost with oil anoint,
and my cup overflows.

6 Goodness and mercy all my life
shall surely follow me:
And in God's house for evermore
my dwelling-place shall be.

Psalms 70

C.M. 8.6.8.6.

1 Make haste, O God, me to preserve;
with speed, Lord, succour me.
2 Let them that for my soul do seek
sham'd and confounded be:

Let them be turned back, and sham'd,
that in my hurt delight.
3 Turn'd back be they, Ha, ha! that say,
their shaming to requite.

4 O Lord, in thee let all be glad,
and joy that seek for thee:
Let them who thy salvation love
say still, God praised be.

5 But I both poor and needy am;
come, Lord, and make no stay:
My help thou and deliv'rer art;
O Lord, make no delay.

Psalms 100

A Psalm of Praises.
L.M. 8.8.8.8.

1 All people that on earth do dwell,
Sing to the Lord with cheerful voice.
2 Him serve with mirth, his praise forth tell,
Come ye before him and rejoice.

3 Know that the Lord is God indeed;
Without our aid he did us make:
We are his flock, he doth us feed,
And for his sheep he doth us take.

4 O enter then his gates with praise,
Approach with joy his courts unto:
Praise, laud, and bless his name always,
For it is seemly so to do.

5 For why? the Lord our God is good,
His mercy is for ever sure;
His truth at all times firmly stood,
And shall from age to age endure.

Psalms 128

A Song of Degrees.
C.M. 8.6.8.6.

1 Bless'd is each one that fears the Lord,
and walketh in his ways;
2 For of thy labour thou shalt eat,
and happy be always.

3 Thy wife shall as a fruitful vine
by thy house' sides be found:
Thy children like to olive-plants
about thy table round.

4 Behold, the man that fears the Lord,
thus blessed shall he be.
5 The Lord shall out of Sion give
his blessing unto thee:

Thou shalt Jerus'lem's good behold
whilst thou on earth dost dwell.
6 Thou shalt thy children's children see,
and peace on Israel.

Psalms 149:1-5, 9

C.M. 8.6.8.6.

1 Praise ye the Lord: unto him sing
a new song, and his praise
In the assembly of his saints
in sweet psalms do ye raise.

2 Let Isr'el in his Maker joy,
and to him praises sing:
Let all that Sion's children are
be joyful in their King.

3 O let them unto his great name
give praises in the dance;
Let them with timbrel and with harp
in songs his praise advance.

4 For God doth pleasure take in those
that his own people be;
And he with his salvation
the meek will beautify.

5 And in his glory excellent
let all his saints rejoice:
Let them to him upon their beds
aloud lift up their voice.

9 On them the judgment to perform
found written in his word:
This honour is to all his saints.
O do ye praise the Lord.

Devotional Suggestions

First, the reading of Robert Murray McCheyne's instruction for use of the "Daily Bread" Scripture readings would be worth reading aloud to the family every now and then. It will remind your family of the dangers and advantages, not only of the scripture readings, but also of the pitfalls and benefits of family devotions in general.

Please keep in mind that the Word of God is that which is of utmost importance in the family devotions. Encourage the private reading of scripture within the family without being overbearing and legalistic. Express to each member of the family the particular joys in the discoveries and illuminations the Holy Spirit brings to God's Word.

Remember that the use of the catechism and the confession of faith are merely tools; moreover, they are tools primarily for the parents rather than the children. Certainly, the reading of a creed and the recitation of the catechism will benefit your children with the Biblical doctrines that the creed and catechism have systematized, categorized, and described; nevertheless, these tools are for *parents* so that the creed and catechism may be frontlets for *your* eyes; so that the Word of God is ever before *your* face, being first upon *your* mind and foremost upon *your* heart; and thus, sweetness to *your* soul. Then, shall your spouse see the love of

God in her husband's life. Then, shall your children see the love of God in their father's life.

The confession of faith need not be the only thing read in the evening. A good book by a reputable and respected author may either substitute or supplement your evening devotions. One very small book that I highly recommend is the treatise written by John Bunyan titled *Christian Behavior. The Pilgrim's Progress* by Mr. Bunyan is also an excellent family devotional supplement.

Reading short biographies of ministers and missionaries will also encourage the family during devotional times.

Seize every opportunity that you are together to be times of devotional worship before the Lord. When you sit at the table for any meal, encourage the memorization of scripture; comment upon that day's scripture reading; ask questions concerning recent scripture readings; encourage your family to ask questions about the portions read.

After having recited your catechism, read your scripture portions, confession of faith, and/or other books, biographies or articles, it would be good to close your family worship with a good classic hymn or a psalm from the Scottish Psalter.

> *See then that ye walk circumspectly, not as fools, but as wise, Redeeming the time, because the days are evil.*
>
> —Ephesians 5:15-16

About the Editor

Jon Cardwell lives in Anniston, Alabama with his wife, Lisa, and his daughter, Rachel. He is the pastor at Sovereign Grace Baptist Church in Anniston after having ministered as a missionary and as a missionary-pastor in the Philippines, California, and remote bush Alaska.

www.justificationbygrace.com

www.sovereigngraceanniston.com

www.vayahiypress.com

jonjcardwell.net

www.facebook.com/christ.crucified

For seminars, workshops or speaking engagements on family devotions, catechizing and worship, you can contact Jon J. Cardwell through:

SOVEREIGN GRACE BAPTIST CHURCH
5440 AL Hwy 202 ~ Anniston, AL 36201
Phone: (256) 275-8996
Email: jon@justificationbygrace.com

BOOKS BY JON J. CARDWELL

A Puritan Bible Primer

For the training of children in preparation for catechizing
in ESV, KJV, NASB & NKJV

A Puritan Family Devotional

is available containing the
1689 LONDON BAPTIST CONFESSION
in ASV, CAMBRIDGE, ESV, GENEVA, KJV, NASB & NKJV

and is also available containing the
WESTMINSTER CONFESSION OF FAITH in KJV

Christ and Him Crucified

Essential Spurgeon

Fullness of the Time

Lord, Teach Us to Pray

FROM VAYAHIY PRESS

edited by Jon J. Cardwell

The Scottish Psalter

Christian Behavior by John Bunyan

Christ as Advocate by John Bunyan

Dying Sayings by John Bunyan

Made in the USA
San Bernardino, CA
24 February 2019